BABY GIRL

Second printing edition 2019
Printed in U.S.A.
Copyright: 2019
All rights reserved
Alvin Bernard Dunston

Alvin Bernard Dunston

BABY GIRL

BABY GIRL

CONTENTS

PREFACE..11

CHAPTER

    I   BABY GIRL...13

    II   MONEY TINA..22

    III   CAPTURED BY A STALKER 30

    IV   GIMME' MY MONEY................................38

    V   ELLEN KIDS ALWAYS STEALIN'..............48

    VI   THE BULLY..58

    VII   THE STONING..78

    VIII   SCHOOL'S CLOSED..................................85

    IX   BABY GIRL'S BIRTHDAY..........................94

    X   THEY KILLED MY DOG..........................102

    XI   CAUGHT CHEATING..............................118

    XII   SHE A HOE..130

    XIII   ELLEN GRADUALLY AWAKENS..............146

    XIV   PAM RETURNS HOME............................158

TO A FAITHFUL HELPER

Fani Miller Beard

DEDICATED TO

Someone special

PREFACE

Baby Girl is based on a true story of survival. The matriarch of the Hendrix family (which consists of six members, the parents and four children) is a seven, year old child named Tina. This is her story. This manuscript covers the years of her life from birth to the age of thirteen. During this time her father abandoned the family and her mother suffered a nervous breakdown as a result of struggling to raise the children alone, and heartbreak. Tina was the oldest child and saved the family by taking their mother's role just when the children needed to be rescued. Her infant sister, Candace, even called her, "Mama," since Tina raised her. Tina bathed, fed and changed Candace's diapers, and carried her on her hip everywhere she went around the house. It was said that Tina was born grown, which is an unfair burden to place on a child, but fortunately for her siblings it was true.

She was forty, four when we met, and a professional working for a non-profit agency that deals with infants, teen mothers, teen fathers, and adult parents. I was surprised when she told me about having no parental guidance as a child. Being able to roam free at such a young age was frightening to me, since I was raised in a loving two, family household, with an over protective mother that was always around, it seemed criminal, and dangerous, not to care for babies. Our conversations came about as innocent correspondence for we had recently met and were getting to know one another. She would often talk about her childhood, and I was astonished at what she told me. I would ask her questions to try and understand her circumstances as a child. She saw I was intrigued and casually answered all of my questions and seemed to remember more as our relationship grew, because she had blocked many things from her mind in order to function productively.

In the text you are about to read how Tina Hendrix endured and triumphed over child abuse. I still do not know how a person can be born grown, so mature as a child, but I have heard the phrase, "Old Soul" mentioned by senior citizens, so I know it's real. I know it's real because Tina is real, and her struggle is real. I was compelled to write about her life. She mentioned her mother always told her it would make a good book. It was a pleasure to communicate to the world, the life of this courageous woman, so that it may inspire other children who are in a similar situation.

Alvin Bernard Dunston
MT. Vernon, NY. February 2019

1

BABY GIRL

She was cold, hungry, and worried about her siblings, as she walked hurriedly in the snow to the corner store. She held the food stamps tightly in her hand, inside her pocket, for she had no gloves to shelter her hands from the wind. She was only seven so she didn't quite understand why her mother stopped moving. She didn't know why her mother stayed in bed all day. She didn't comprehend why her mother sat on the sofa chewing crushed ice, not talking, frighteningly staring at the television. All she knew was that she was hungry and had to eat. She was confident as she scampered down the street, for she had done this before. She knew the grocer and recognized the sadness in his eyes. She knew he pitied her and would not deny her purchase, even though he should have, because she was a baby. She was a little caramel colored baby girl. She had a cute face and button shaped nose with fat cheeks and big brown eyes. She was short for her age, and chubby, and the grocer adored her, but he had three kids of his own to feed so all he could do was be nice to the little princess, and occasionally slip a few extra items into her bag.

As Baby Girl entered the store she looked to the floor, kept her head down, and quietly gathered items from the aisles. She heard loud voices as she moved about and realized the shouting was from an argument. She had to shop quickly because her brother and sisters were waiting for her. She approached the counter and saw it was the grocer yelling at a customer. She bravely decided to yell too.

"Excuse me Mr. Sir! Mr. Sir! I'm ready."

The grocer paused and looked confused for he didn't see his precious enter the store. He still couldn't see her now and had to lean over the register to gaze upon her. He frowned and said,

"Now what I tell ya' bout' comin' in here by yo' self? Next time ya' betta' git' someone ta' help ya' carry dat."

"Yes sir Mr. Sir" she replied.

Baby Girl held a basket filled with food but couldn't lift it to the counter so the grocer reached down and grabbed it from her.

"Didn't your mother teach you not to interrupt when grownups are talkin?" asked the customer, sternly, which upset the grocer, and Baby Girl was startled as he angrily ordered the customer to leave the store.

"You no account deadbeat! Get the hell outta' here!" he screamed, then took a deep breath, regained his composer and whispered to his princess.

"My dear, please bring someone with you next time. It's not safe out here. These crazy fools will snatch you. I sho' wish I could keep you with my family but my wife would have a fit. Here, I put an extra loaf in dare' and some candy fo' y'all. You be careful now."

Baby Girl walked briskly with the wind on her back and a heavy, brown paper grocery bag, in each hand. The milk weighed the most and caused her shoulders to slump but she was a strong little girl and struggled to reach her home. Her shoes were worn and her clothes were tattered. The handles from the weight of the bags made red marks on her hands and wrist but she only stopped once to rest. Upon reaching home she put the bags on the kitchen table, removed her coat, and sat quietly as she removed her shoes and unpacked the groceries. She was mentally and physically drained, and wanted to rest before retrieving her youngest sibling, her baby sister who she treated like her daughter.

There were four children in the Hendrix family. Baby Girl was the oldest child, being seven. She had two sisters and a brother. Pam was five, Herby was three, and Candace was thirteen months. Baby Girl assumed the role of mother after their own mother shut down. She was a responsible caregiver and knew when to be bossy. She was too young to realize she was saving her siblings. She only knew that she loved her baby sister and brother. She did everything for them. She changed her sister's diapers, and fed her, and carried her on her hip everywhere around the house. She had no guidance or supervision since her mother's breakdown, and she enjoyed this freedom, it was exciting. Luckily for her family, she was a naturally caring and responsible child. If she had been like her younger sister the family would not have survived, because Pam, the five, year old, was selfish and deceitful. She was a liar and a thief, and enjoyed being this way. She thought of Baby Girl as a fool, as an obstacle and didn't appreciate her taking their mother's place, since she let her do whatever she wanted. It was fun at first, being the mom, but it was tiresome now because Baby Girl was a child and wanted to be taken care of too. She wanted to have lullabies sung to her at bedtime, and awaken to a warm meal like she did before her father left, when her mother was loving.

Baby Girl liked to cook, so she turned on the stove and opened the oven door to warm herself in the heat. There was a faint smell of gas in the air as she went to retrieve Candace. She let her other siblings sleep as she gently woke the baby. She could smell urine in the diaper and knew it needed to be changed. She instinctively retrieved a fresh diaper, a hand towel, powder, then changed her. She excitedly carried Candace to the kitchen and sat her in the highchair in front of the stove. She was happy because it was Monday and she loved school, and couldn't wait to show her favorite teacher the homework she completed over the weekend.

After putting her school supplies and books into her backpack, she picked out her siblings' clothes. She knew she had plenty of time, the result of always waking early, a trait she learned from her mother before the breakdown. She always bathed her siblings at night, which made her morning preparations easier. She would fill the tub to bathe alone but Pam and Herby always interrupted her by bursting into the bathroom and jumping in the tub with their toys; she hated that.

"Get up and get them clothes on!" She screamed and smacked Pam on the backside. Her sister yelled, and faked crying.

"Stop hittin' me," she said, and rose from the bed slowly and proceeded to dress. She was glad they all shared the same bedroom for it made things easier. They lived in a three, bedroom home in the Dayton Metropolitan Public Houses. Their mother had her own bedroom while Baby Girl and Pam shared a room. Herby and Candace shared the third bedroom which was the smallest; but their room stayed empty because it was always cold and their mother feared spirits lived there, believing that ghost can only survive in the cold.

"I can't go ta' school today. I don't feel well," Pam whined.

"You feel just fine. The only reason you don't want to go is because you didn't do your homework. I told you to do it but all you wanna' do is watch T.V. and play. You so lazy."

"Shut up!"

"No, you shut up and get in that kitchen so we can eat!"

Cold cereal was for breakfast. It was quick and easy and Baby Girl just bought a gallon of milk and a big box of Frosted Flakes. Pam didn't like the cereal and began to fuss. This happened so many times in the past that she had to buy her siblings different cereal. Pam liked Cocoa Puffs and Herby liked Fruit Loops. She learned quickly to appease them if she wanted things to go smoothly, so she automatically retrieved the boxes of cereal and gave each child their favorite. Her mother was awake now and entered the kitchen. Without saying a word or looking at her children, she walked to the refrigerator and filled her cup with ice. She walked like a zombie, like so many of the dead spirits she was afraid of. She walked to the living room and sat on the couch chewing the ice, continuously crunching, staring off into the distance. She was numb to her mother's demeanor because she had been this way for so long. She couldn't be distracted if she wanted to get to school on time, knowing Pam would drag her feet the whole way.

It was a constant battle between Baby Girl and Pam. One child was good and the other child was evil. It was hard to believe they shared the same parents since the sisters had so drastically different personalities. They shared many things in common physically, because of their DNA but their mentalities were different. Pam was smart, but she used her intelligence for evil. She used her intellect to lie, steal and manipulate people. They were also different morally. Different morals and values separated the sisters because their mother possessed both nurturing qualities and devious traits, exposing them to her daughters separately.

Baby Girl was exposed to her mother's nurturing side, before her father abandoned them. She was the first born so she experienced the love her mother possessed for her father. It was a deep love and her mother wanted to please him with their first child. She wanted a boy because she knew that would make him happy, but since he welcomed their daughter unconditionally, she was overjoyed and focused on her wellbeing.

Pam was born two years after Baby Girl, when her twenty, year old mother's mind was declining due to stress from worrying about their father, who was running the streets with reckless abandonment, while coming and going at all times of the day and night. He was eighteen now and pimping girls while traveling the neighborhood to collect his money. He was abusing drugs and alcohol, and believed he passed these chemicals to Pam through birth, contributing to her destructive behavior.

Pam experienced a different side of her mother, but it wasn't loving it was tolerant, it wasn't caring it was dutiful. As time moved on, she witnessed the fits of rage that her mother displayed due to her father's absence, and heard her curse him to hell. Pam was attracted to this side of her mother and grew jealous of Baby Girl because she was not subjected to this behavior. Everything was sanitized and all behavior was morally just in her presence. She was shielded from the ugly things and Pam knew this was a lie. She knew her mother and father were acting this way to make Baby Girl think everything was okay. Pam resented the fact that she wasn't considered good enough to be lied to. It seemed like it was alright to curse and fuss in her presence. Pam learned most of her behavior from her parent's destructive interactions. She saw how they gave her sister things, and felt she was not being treated fairly, so she had no problem morally, when she stole little things that she believed were due. She had no remorse telling lies because she had seen her parents lie to each other so often. She couldn't wait to lie, steal and make people cry. Causing people misery pleased her.

The children's father was a short, plump, light skinned handsome man whose mother ran a number joint. His family had old money. They were accustomed to new cars, jewels, furs and real estate. To be fashionable, rich, and famous was what he wanted too. He liked the fame most of all. Their mother met this handsome, flashy man and was overwhelmed with emotion, gradually giving him her heart. Eventually she realized that she couldn't keep him happy, or home, for the streets were in his blood. He only stayed because she portrayed herself as a religious and wholesome girl. His mother knew different because she was older and knew the history of the Hendrix family. She grew up with the grandmother and knew she was the religious one who brought the family to church every Sunday, and this was known in the community, pleasing their father because he didn't want a fast girl from the streets as his mate, although he didn't mind having one for his pleasure.

Their mother had worldly thoughts about lust and desire, even though she went to church. Eventually she was approached by this fifteen, year old boy. She admired his clothes and attractive features. She admired the purple Cadillac he drove and the suave friends that surrounded him. He informed her about an older lady that was courting him, who drove a white mustang convertible, gave him money, and bought him things, but he didn't want her as a mate because he didn't trust her, intriguing Baby Girl's mother since she had never been the object of someone's affection. Being seventeen and naive she was not equipped to defend against his advances, and soon had no desire to. She liked the fact that he had money and was an independent lad. She overlooked him doing illegal things because he began to buy her clothes and take care of her. He took her on road trips to different states and made her feel special. By the time her mother learned of the affair with this street hustler, it was too late for she was pregnant. Her mother nearly died from the betrayal and was ashamed. Being a religious woman, she wanted to make things right with the Lord. She believed, in God's eyes, the young couple wouldn't be sinners if they were covered in JESUS blood by matrimony, but this wasn't meant to be. Her father was not given permission to marry because his mother objected. She didn't approve of her only son marrying an older woman, even if it was only by two years. Big Mama, as she was known in the community, was not about to have her precious son married off so young. She agreed to help him take care of his daughter but that was all.

    In the Hendrix family, the power lay on her father's side, in the hands of the women. Big Mama carried a pistol and shot a few men during the years of owning and running her business, a three, family mansion on the south side of Dayton Ohio. It was a brothel, juke joint and numbers house. She drove a purple Cadillac, the same one her son borrowed to impress his friends, and wore an assortment of fur coats as she traveled around town. Her sister had a restaurant on the same street, and the two women shared customers and money while amassing a fortune equal to or better than anyone in town.

    When Baby Girl's father left, the family slowly declined into poverty. I say left, but really, he just never returned. It happened gradually. First, he stayed away one night, then one weekend, then one week, until finally he never returned. He was still in town of course, enjoying his fast life while forgetting about his obligations to his children. When the youngest child was just a newborn he was gone, leaving their mother with four mouths to feed. The responsibility of raising the children was too much for her. She tried to keep up appearances at first, but soon she was behind on the rent and ashamed to ask his family for help, losing the house instead. Finally, some family members did take them in, but times were hard and since she didn't work, Big Mama wasn't about to pay their rent, and advised her to apply for welfare. She said they would be a priority because of the children. She said welfare would get them an apartment and food stamps. Her mother didn't want to go because she was accustomed to being cared for by their father and didn't want to struggle alone. She secretly hoped he would return once he heard how bad things were, but he never did, and the time came when the family had to move again; this time, from a nice home with relatives to the Dayton Metropolitan Public Houses.

The public houses were separated into different sections with each area having a name. The first section the family moved to was called Desoto Bass. It was the worst section of Dayton where crime was rampant, shootings and murders were widespread, drugs were sold daily as dealers terrorized the people and recruited the young boys for their gangs. Her mother was still confident because she was only weeks removed from suburban life, but after six months living in Desoto was unbearable, and frightening, and compounded her depression. Luckily, she was still well enough to relocate the family to another section of public housing called Hilltop, which was less dangerous. Moving the family was her last constructive act before shutting down completely. Fortunately, she had an older relative, Uncle Stanley, who helped her.

Stanley understood his niece was suffering a mental breakdown because he had seen it before. As a teenager he witnessed the debilitating effect that occurs when a person's mind is broken. He knew a school mate that killed himself because of a girl. It happened gradually, after they broke up. His friend became withdrawn, unsociable, and over time his condition worsened until his demeanor was that of a stranger. Stanley could still remember thinking his friend was just sad, it was a phase he was going through, soon his personality would return and he would be okay, but it never happened, and to his agony and disbelief, his friend jumped head first from the top of the bleachers in the high school gymnasium, breaking his neck. Some students said it was an accident, that he slipped, but Stanley suspected the worst, and when a letter was found in his friend's room confessing his eternal love for his beloved, it was confirmed. Stanley never forgot the feeling of guilt he experienced because he wasn't helpful to his friend. He didn't realize the severity of the situation and this haunted him, causing him to have nightmares, compelling him to make a vow to never again disregard a friend's emotions, therefore, when everyone in his family turned their back on his niece, saying she was crazy, he was willing to help, but he had zero tolerance for deceit, and laziness.

After Baby Girl's father abandoned them, it was Stanley who bought them a used car and some furniture, and helped them move to Hilltop. He was watchful of his niece's life now, when before he observed from afar. Stanley witnessed his niece stop caring for her children. He knew her mate had gone and immediately associated her circumstances with his childhood friend since they both had been heartbroken. Stanley couldn't endure the thought of observing another suicide, or seeing his niece abuse drugs and alcohol to medicate her sadness, so he helped her just when she needed assistance the most. When depression rendered her unable to initiate contact, or reach out to him, he voluntarily visited after his sister threw her out of the house. Stanley followed them from place to place, visiting twice a month at first, but now that her mind regressed, and removed her desire to function, he visited several times a week.

Stanley supported Baby Girl when he saw how smart she was. It was said that she was born grown, which is an unfair burden to place on an infant, but her mother did. As soon as she realized her daughter could care for her siblings, she selfishly placed them in her care, making her run the household. Who would do such a thing? Who would let a seven, year old freely roam the streets shopping for the family, it was shocking and unbelievable, but in the area where they lived no one questioned it, so it came to be that this special child was allowed to purchase whatever she needed from the local stores without the accompaniment of an adult. She was known as Lil bit, from Hilltop. Gradually the store owners welcomed her because at least they knew her purchases were legitimate since she possessed government food stamps. The store owners protected her as much as they could and were sympathetic because they knew it was unfair to send a child so young to run errands.

Stanley often scolded his niece when she didn't take care of her children, but he wasn't severe because he knew her mind was fragile. Still, he was encouraged by Baby Girl's progress in school and always came to see her report card. He was impressed with her grades for she was an "A" student, and he knew with the proper guidance she would survive being neglected. He would bring a gift, and call her out to his car every time she received a report card, which was four times a year. He rarely entered the house when he came to see her, only if he needed to speak with her mother, whose condition had worsened, keeping her from venturing out. She looked forward to his visits and was happy to have someone see her grades, since her mother was unconcerned. Stanley was the only one besides her teacher that encouraged her to be successful in school. She liked their encouragement, she liked being smart and was proud of her accomplishments, but still she wished her mother was happy and caring, like before, when the family was together.

II

MONEY TINA

It was July 1969, and Ellen was in labor. Her mother accompanied her to Miami Valley Hospital in Dayton, Ohio, and stayed with her along with the doctor and nurses as her first born quickly ejected into his hands. The doctor was surprised and almost dropped the baby for he did not expect it to emerge so fast, even though he was experienced and had performed many births. The newborn was slippery, and the doctor immediately gave it to one of the nurses as the after birth discharged. He cut the umbilical cord and smacked the baby's bottom before sitting the infant on Ellen's chest. Ellen cried while her mother looked on, rubbing her shoulders, expressionless. When the doctor and nurses left the room, her expression changed to worry. She was a religious woman and was concerned, not because she had another mouth to feed, but because she wondered how this could happen when she was so careful to raise her seventeen, year old daughter right, in the LORDS way, after all she did take Ellen to church every Sunday, and instilled in her the morals and values of a good Christian woman.

    Thirty minutes passed before the doctor and nurses returned, placed the baby into a bassinet then took it away. The nurses rolled Ellen's bed down the hallway into an elevator and brought her back to the maternity ward on the third floor. They told her the infant would be taken to the nursery with the rest of the newborns, and she could go there after they cleaned it. Various nurses entered and exited her room, examining and washing her vagina, and stomach, and dressing her in a new hospital gown as Ellen's mother observed. The Senior nurse came into the room with some papers for them to fill out, asking if she had any allergic reactions to certain foods, or Penicillin, and various questions about the father of the child, asking if Ellen wanted the baby to have his last name. Ellen answered yes but the nurse knew she couldn't approve without the father's consent, still she listed Elmore James, as the biological.

    When it was time for Ellen to see her daughter, she slowly

walked with her mother down the hallway to the nursery. She was surprised to see about twenty newborn babies there, but soon she located her child by reading the names on the different bassinets. She was happy because they sat her daughter in the first row by the glass, and she gazed upon her, unhindered by distance since the babies were assembled four rows deep. The two nurses in the room wore face masks and gladly carried the children to the window, and held them to the glass so the many families that were assembled could have a closer look. The families smiled, waved, and made faces at the babies. It was a joyous occasion until Big Mama showed up and confronted Ellen's mother, Eunice.

    Big Mama wanted to see her grandchild since it was her only son's child. She wanted the baby to live with her so she could provide for it. Because she was wealthy, she believed she could care for the baby better than Eunice and Ellen.

    "Where my grandbaby at!" she yelled as she strolled regally down the hallway like a queen, with her royal blue fox coat draped over her shoulders. She had already handed her matching fur clutch purse, which was specially made, to her assistant, who was a thin, young, timid looking girl with a pecan complexion and wavy auburn hair. The girl was taller than Big Mama and stood quietly behind her ready to hold her coat, because she had been in this situation before and knew the procedure. The girl knew if her boss was going to fight, she would throw her coat off, and she had to be ready to catch it.

    "Now which baby is it? Where my grandbaby at? Lawd, they got so many babies here!" she exclaimed as she approached Eunice and Ellen.

    "You know I don't like you," she said with a frown as she looked at Ellen, while ignoring Eunice.

    "Now don't you start no mess in here. You know I'm a Christian," Eunice replied.

    "Huh, Christian my ass. You may be a Christian but your daughter ain't. Sleepin' round' like dat!" exclaimed Big Mama. Since her father was white and her mother was native American, she expected her grandchild to be a reddish beige, or yellow complexion, but seeing the nurse hold up a light brown child, she had her doubts.

    "I ain't been sleepin' round'. Your son's the only one I been wit!" Ellen cried.

"Bullshit! How I know that's even my sons' child. Imma' take her wit' me and when she's old enough we gonna' get a blood test!"

"You crazy if you think you takin' that baby anywhere!" Eunice yelled for she could no longer control her temper.

"The devil is a lie!" she screamed. "I rebuke you devil! You ain't nuthin' but the devil! Sataaaan! I rebuke you Satan! The devil is a lie!" Eunice screamed, and made such a fuss that the hospital orderlies had to come and separate the women. They ordered Big Mama to leave and followed her to the exit as her assistant accompanied them, carrying her belongings. Ellen was surprised by the altercation between the two grandmothers, but she wasn't angry with Big Mama, though she disliked her, she still wanted to live in luxury, not wanting to struggle, knowing if she lived in Big Mama's house all her needs would be fulfilled since she possessed the one thing Big Mama desired, a grandchild.

The next morning the nurses and doctor visited Ellen's room several times to make sure she was bonding with her daughter. They were encouraged because Eunice was an experienced mother and showed Ellen how to hold, feed, and burp the newborn. By the afternoon the nurses and doctor were confident enough to release the family, and accompanied them to the exit as they rolled Ellen in a wheel chair, which was the normal procedure. Eunice and Ellen didn't smile as they entered a taxi, which was unusual because new parents were commonly seen laughing and joyfully smiling when they departed the hospital.

The newborn child was named, Tina Hendrix. She had her mother's last name because Big Mama wouldn't let them use her name, just in case her son wasn't the father. She still wanted the baby to live with her because she couldn't stand the thought of a potential relative being raised elsewhere, after all, she had a reputation to uphold. Any grandchild of hers would be spoiled, and pampered, and treated to the finer things in life, things Eunice and Ellen couldn't provide. Her desire to obtain the baby consumed her and she was unable to control her emotions. As soon as her son returned home, she convinced him to accompany her to Ellen's house to take the baby. Big Mama said she would let them stay on the third floor of her mansion. Her son liked this because he knew the apartment on that floor was spacious. He currently lived in the bedroom he grew up in, on the second floor, and knew it wasn't big enough for Ellen and his child to live comfortably.

Big Mama sped to Eunice's house accompanied by her son, with her pistol stored in the glove compartment. She always carried her gun because it was a dangerous life she lived, running numbers, and a brothel, and a juke joint, which caused her to meet all kinds of men, and sometimes they tried to cheat her since she was a woman. She proved that she could protect herself, and her reputation was that of a strong, brave, no-nonsense woman.

Ellen and Eunice reached home that afternoon and by the evening they heard a loud knock on the door and were surprised to be ambushed by Big Mama, who burst through the door as soon as it was opened, and waved her pistol at the women while demanding her grandchild. Eunice was afraid for she had never experienced such a thing, and ran toward the back of the house to her daughter's room to protect the baby. When Ellen realized what was happening, she quickly packed a few things and ran toward the door to her mother's dismay. Eunice was angry that her daughter was so willing to leave and she screamed, and yelled for help, and tried to stop her by pulling the baby from her arms, but when Big Mama pointed the pistol at her, she had no choice but to let them leave with her grandchild, whom she had only known for forty, eight hours.

The first two years of Baby Girl's life were traumatic. Even though she lived with her father's family in comfort, and elegance, she was unprotected from him. The father, Jamison Lemmon, was called Baby Fats, and he loved being in the streets. He loved riding up and down the block in his mother's fancy car as an assortment of friends accompanied him everywhere. Fifth Street was where he hung out and it was where all the prostitutes, pimps, and hustlers were. Baby Fats dressed sharp and stayed on the strip, which ran for several miles, because he aspired to be a pimp and hustler too. His mother's mansion lay on the corner of Shannon, street, just three blocks from Fifth Street. The young ladies loved him because he was a handsome, light skinned man, with wavy black hair they called, "The Butters", and he was Big Mama's son.

Big Mama was busy operating her business and transformed her mansion into a juke joint, before her son was born, where illegal numbers were played. The first floor was a parlor where her guest congregated. There were soft burgundy leather couches and beautiful stained, glass windows, adorned with burgundy velvet drapes reaching to the top of the high, rise ceiling. Stylish glass ash trays and beautiful wooden coasters sat on round mahogany tables so her guest could smoke, and drink freely as they socialized with her girls. If a patron wanted a private room, they would go upstairs to the second floor where seven rooms of various sizes could be used for sex. The price of the rooms depended on the size, and duration of ones stay, which ranged from thirty minutes to an hour. Only special guest with long money could stay overnight, and the largest room was reserved for that, because it contained a bed, sofa, and a table and chair set. Big Mama was a fair Madam for she let her girls keep a quarter of the money they earned, as opposed to the pimps on Fifth street who took everything, keeping their prostitutes penniless and dependent. The money for the room was paid directly to Big Mama, leaving the whore free to negotiate her own price for service. There was usually a standard price for sex, but some girls who were fancy charged their johns higher prices.

      The bar was located in the rear of the first floor behind two large sliding oak doors, with figures of women and men dancing carved into the woodwork. This was the area where everyone let loose, and liquor controlled their inhibitions, accompanied by the blues music that blasted from the jukebox, and caused them to lie, cheat, gamble, and commit adultery. The blues and liquor had everyone spellbound with its' sordid tales of lost love and fornication.

      Baby Fats loved his daughter and wanted to spend time with her, but he wasn't accustomed to raising an infant, so he thought it was amusing when he put beer in her bottle to make her go to sleep at night. He thought it was funny when he showed his toddler how to smoke weed when she was only two years old. He put her on display like show and tell at school, so his friends could see since they didn't believe she could blow marijuana smoke through her nose, and they laughed with approval every time she did.

      Baby Girl was helpless to her father's abuse, and Ellen was unconcerned because she was in the early stages of her depression, caused by his ever, increasing drug use, and his need to recruit more girls to work the streets for him. Ellen suspected him of being unfaithful and was afraid of losing her beloved, so she did all she could to please him. She noticed how his sexual needs became more perverted, but still she complied even though some of the things he did to her where unwanted and painful. She felt compelled to satisfy his sexual desires because she knew the street walkers that worked for him would gladly do all he asked. At first it was hard for her to accept his chosen occupation because she didn't want a pimp for a mate, but as the money accumulated and he took care of her every need, she gradually relaxed because she believed he truly loved her.

    Big Mama called her precious grandbaby, Money Tina, ever since she sat her on the end of the bar one New Year's Eve, dressed in a red Casmir jumpsuit, and marveled at the sight of all her guests, stuffing money into the toddler's pockets as they merrily drank and partied. Since that time, she made it a habit of sitting her there. She was surprised to see how everyone loved giving her money and playing with her. Baby Girl was too young to remember that she stayed on the bar under Big Mama's watchful eye until she fell asleep, which sometimes didn't occur until two or three in the morning. Big Mama didn't know the second, hand smoke filling Baby Girl's lungs was harmful, for people at this time didn't know it was dangerous. All she knew was that her grandbaby was making money at two years old, and she giggled with approval at the end of the night as she counted the bills with delight, for they always amounted to more than fifty dollars. Big Mama laughed to herself and sometimes exclaimed outright, "See my grandbaby makin' more money than people at a regular job!"

    She was a fixture in the bar during her second and third year of life, until one fateful night when a patron got too comfortable with her, and Big Mama finally realized a bar is no place for a toddler to be, amongst drunks, prostitutes, gamblers and thieves. On this particular night, since she was old enough to walk, she left her post at the end of the bar to venture out, when she realized no one was watching her. After Big Mama stepped away to go upstairs and confront an unruly customer, Baby Girl climbed down off the bar and walked to the front parlor, past the large sliding oak doors, for they were partially open and she was able to squeeze through. She sat on a large sofa with three other women who were socializing with some men they met. As the night progressed the couples gradually left, leaving her sitting alone in the corner of the sofa by the armrest. A strange man approached her and stuffed a dollar in her shirt while laying his head on her lap. At first, she was startled because his head was heavy and wet with sweat. She wanted to move but the man had fallen asleep and she was trapped under the weight of his head. There were other people in the room who continued to drink and party, unaware of what was happening. After an hour passed the man began to snore and Baby Girl started to whine with disapproval, and tried to lift his head off her lap but it was too heavy. Another thirty minutes passed and she was distraught now, since no one came to her aid, to remove the man, so she began to cry, squirm, and kick her feet to no avail. It was too much for her to bare, this strange man with wet hair, sleeping with his heavy head on her lap, she was terrified and trapped so she let out a loud scream, but the music was too loud and everyone was drunk so no one noticed her distress. Finally, another drunk man sat on the couch next to them and noticed the strange man with his head on her lap and realized she was trapped. He saw her crying and hit the man several times to wake him, unsuccessfully. Luckily, he alerted one of the girls in the room and she came over with another woman, and dragged the stranger by his feet, sending him tumbling off the sofa, freeing her from beneath him. Her lap was wet from the man's sweaty head and she continued to cry. Big Mama appeared just in time to see the confrontation and slapped the strange man, then ordered him to leave, then she scooped Baby Girl into her arms and held her tight, promising her little princess that she would never have her sitting on the bar again collecting money.

    She received her first fur coat soon after that frightful incidence because Big Mama had another use for her. She wanted to spend time away from her mansion of ill repute, since that was the only way, she could guarantee the child's safety and still have fun, so she took Baby Girl along to the boxing matches at the stadium downtown called the Hara Arena. It was an event she attended for years, every Friday night accompanied by her man, Big Papa. She would get in her purple Cadillac Seville and go to the fights, wearing her finest dress and her mink coat. It was only Baby Girl's second time going with them and she liked dressing up and riding to the city. She sat in the front seat on the armrest in between the two adults. There were no child seats in 1973, and it wasn't unlawful to travel with a baby roaming about the vehicle without a seatbelt. She was excited as she watched the landscape change from a country setting to the bright lights and concrete buildings of the city.

    Big Mama was delighted because her grandbaby was like a miniature version of herself. They were dressed alike, with the same accessories and matching fur coats. It was a sight to behold when the two of them traveled together, and Big Mama loved this because she always wanted to be famous. Strangers would point and stare and some would even take pictures of them for it was rare to see a toddler wearing a mink coat. On this particular night they happened to be attending a championship fight, and the arena was filled to capacity. The crowd looked on with curiosity as they wondered who this royal lady was sitting ringside. They saw Big Papa, and the child sitting in the seat between them, wearing matching fur coats, and figured Big Mama must be a celebrity.

  The main event was at the end of the evening with three fights before it. Baby Girl was bored and sat quietly in her seat as Big Mama and Papa cheered the fighters on, whistling and applauding as the boxers battled in the ring. She was happy to eat her treats and drink the soda they bought her, but after the first fight and before the second one started, a group of midgets climbed into the ring and she immediately froze since she had never seen a grown man so small. She marveled at how they wobbled about the ring wearing big red oversized gloves and shiny black trunks. When the bell rang, they all converged upon the center of the ring, swinging wildly at each other, and she dropped her treats, stood up in her chair and started throwing punches in the air too, mimicking the pint, sized men. Big Mama screamed with delight upon seeing her grandbaby boxing. She cheered and clapped and even got the crowd involved as she screamed, "That's my Grandbaby! Punch em', punch em' good baby!"

  Now Baby Girl was having fun, and laughed as she imitated the little men punching each other, and she almost fell from her seat as each man was knocked down, one by one, until only the winner remained standing. At the end of the fight the winner raised his hands and jumped about the ring and she raised her hands too. She was happy and excited and repeated her actions as the evening progressed. Each time the midgets came out she copied them, throwing punches from her seat, marveling at the spectacle, and making Big Mama proud.

III

CAPTURED BY A STALKER WHEN FORGOTTEN

At the age of four, Baby Girl had a brown fox fur coat and a black mink. Aside from going to the fights with Big Mama she also accompanied her father during the day as he went about his routine of parlaying with his whores, and selling drugs. His drug use included cocaine now, when before he only smoked marijuana and drank alcohol. It was because of money that he even encountered the drug. He saw how most of the johns sniffed coke, so he figured it was a natural progression to sell the drug along with his girls. Like Big Mama, Fats liked the attention he received when he traveled with his daughter for, she always wore fancy outfits.

One this particular day she sat on the arm rest in the front seat of the Cadillac. It was Saturday, collection day, and Candy sat next to her as Fats drove down Fifth street. Candy was fussing with Baby Girl's brown fox coat. She liked the feel of the fluffy fur on her finger tips and stroked Baby Girls' shoulder and arm as if she were a pet. Candy was envious because the short rabbit fur she wore wasn't glamorous like the full, length, fox. Candy was tall, shapely, and young, with a yellowish tan complexion, and curly, ox blood, hair, crowned her head, accompanied by crimson freckles. Her attractive smile and hazel eyes established her as Fats main girl, and the only one allowed to ride in the front seat with him, but Fats didn't want her to touch his precious daughter and scolded her.

"What I tell you bout' rubbin' on her like dat! She ain't no damn Chihuahua."

"I'm sorry baby," Candy replied, and stopped stroking Baby Girl's arm but she kept her hand on the coat. She was unaware of her actions for the fur had seduced her, and she only removed her hand when Fats raised his fist.

"You heard what I said!" he yelled, and angrily stared at her.

Now, Candy was sad and sulked as she sank into the soft leather seat of the Cadillac, and frowned from the disappointing texture of her rabbit fur.

"You seen Ebony?"

"I saw her yesterday."

"Did I ask you bout' yesta' day? I know she hidin' from me. We gonna' drive round' till' we find her. See, you can't leave her wit' no money. You gotta' git' her money at the end of the night. I try ta' be nice but she always actin' up." Candy didn't respond because she was still upset that Fats hadn't bought her a nice fur.

"You hear me talkin' girl?" he asked, and tried to make eye contact but Baby Girl obstructed his view as she played with the soft, spongy, oversized dice hanging from the rearview mirror.

"I hear you but we can't go everywhere with your daughter. Some places we can't take her. You know Ebony might be over at Black's house."

"Das' right. Nah', I ain't takin' her over there. Dem' fools is crazy. Dey' be shootin' too. I would take her back home but my mama gone and my lady gonna' want me ta' stay."

On this sunny Saturday in early May, Baby Fat's mind was influenced by the nice weather as he drove to Riverview Park, a popular place with two basketball courts, baseball fields. a tennis court, and fields of beautiful grass adorned with large wooden gazebos, where many people held their family reunions. He was high, and his mind convinced him that it would be okay to leave Baby Girl in the park awhile. Fat's reasoning was, his daughter would get to play with the other kids because he was taking her to the area in the park where an enormous shelter was located. This installation had a sliding board, fireman poles, monkey bars and swings of various shapes and sizes. Many children were already playing when they arrived, so Fats felt comfortable as he leisurely walked her to the apparatus, knelt down, gave her a five, dollar bill and kissed her on the cheek.

"I'll be back soon. You stay here and play, and if you want something you can git' it from duh food truck, okay." She smiled when she took the money for it reminded her of when she would sit on the bar at Big Mama's house and people would give her tips. She was happy as she skipped toward the jungle gym to play with the other children, and Fats was relieved because now he could freely search for Ebony.

"I'm hungry baby," Candy replied when Fats returned to the

car.

"We'll git' something ta' eat at duh' diner as soon as we git' back on the scene."

"Good, I'm starving. We might even see Ebony there. She go there sometimes."

"I doubt it. She know I'm lookin' for her. Our best bet is Black house, like you said, but I don't wanna' get there too early. They don't even wake up till' round' one, anyway."

Baby Girl stood out from the other kids because she wore a fur coat and it was unusual to see a child playing in such expensive clothing. Some kids laughed and pointed when they saw her coming down the sliding board, while others were curious and touched her coat, rubbing it like Candy had done. She didn't want to be touched so she ran to the other end of the Jungle Gym to get away from them, but one boy kept following her because he liked her. She thought he was annoying and punched him every time he touched her. He was undeterred and only stopped harassing her when his mother saw what was happening and intervened. She grabbed her son by the hand and forcefully lead him away from the structure, scolding him before releasing her grasp.

As she played, she was unaware of the time and only noticed the day was progressing when she had to use the lavatory. She didn't know it was five o'clock in the afternoon, she didn't know she had been in the park for six hours because she was only four and had no concept of time, but she did notice many of the children had gone. She scanned the area in search of the restroom as she stood in the bell tower, which was the highest point of the shelter. She had a good view and located a brick house in the distance. She watched as men and boys walked in one door and women and girls entered another, so she figured it must be the bathroom. She climbed down and walked to the building unaware of the looks and stares from every adult she passed. Most were silently amused at the sight of the little princess in her brown fox fur coat, and forest green, alligator skin, ballerina slippers. Some adults even giggled outright and waved, because most ladies wished they had worn a beautiful fur and elegant dress when they were four years old. No one seemed alarmed seeing the child alone because they figured her parents, or family members had to be nearby.

She was walking slowly and didn't notice one lady in particular watching her every move. The lady was standing at the door to the bathroom and smiled when Baby Girl approached. The lady was the only one who found it odd that the child was alone, and scanned the area when she walked past to see if any adults were guarding her, but she didn't notice anyone. In disbelief she was compelled to investigate. She was discrete as she followed her back to the jungle gym and watched, spellbound, as Baby Girl played. She was amazed to see her enchantment so mature and confident as she skipped to the ice cream truck to get some treats. She saw that Baby Girl had money and smiled because the little girl acted like a lady.

    The strange woman ignored her own children who were older, and nearby, to gaze upon this china doll, imagining the child was her. She always dreamt of being a princess as a little girl, so the sight of a real, life princess enslaved her mind, and caused her to have malicious thoughts about abduction. She was envious because she had an unhappy childhood. Her parents were poor and couldn't afford expensive things. The lady mistook their poverty for uncaring, but she was wrong. Even though her parents were poor they still cared for her deeply. She marveled at the vision of her extravagant doll, and only wished Baby Girl wore a tiara to complete the image in her fantasy.

    The stalker had three children in the park, two daughters and a son, ages eight, nine and eleven, who played around a grill that was nearby and didn't notice their mother's absence until they were hungry. They excitedly approached their mother together. They were happy to run free on such a pleasant day and were surprised at her indifference to their demands.

    "Mama, the food is ready! Daddy wants you to clear the grill and set the table so we can eat."

    She ignored her children and abruptly ran to the shelter because her enchantment was hurt. The lady observed as her muse slipped off the monkey bars and injured herself. She was pleased because no one noticed the incident so she was the only one to come to her aid. Baby Girl hit her head on one of the wooden posts when she fell, and quietly whimpered as she sat in the sand. Because she was injured, she welcomed the friendly, caring, strange lady. The stalker breathed deeply as she hugged her princess and couldn't stop herself from stroking the fur. Every time she rubbed Baby Girl's coat the stalker let out a soft, simmering, sigh, that would have been awkward to anyone but a child, so she didn't notice. She was just happy to be held, and relaxed in the stranger's arms, then fell asleep.

By now the stalker's family was ready to leave because it was getting dark. Her husband found her beneath the Jungle Gym and was upset because he had been looking for her.

"Woman! You betta' get yo' ass out here! I been lookin' all over for you!"

"Baby, we can't just leave her here," the stalker replied.

"Who you talkin' bout?" her husband asked, and peered into the setting sun to see his wife holding what he thought was a little baby deer, when he saw the brown fur, but when his eyes adjusted, he could see that she was holding an angel.

"Where you git' her from?" he asked.

"Baby, she's all alone. I don't know where her parents at."

"I'm not alone mister. She won't lemme' go," Baby Girl revealed.

"Whatchu' talkin' bout' little girl," the man asked since he was confused.

"I told her I'm waitin' for my daddy but she won't lemme' go," she answered, and struggled to free herself so the man could see she was being detained.

"Woman… is you crazy! You know nobody gonna' leave that beautiful chil' alone. Let her go!"

"I can't leave her here. You don't know. I been watching her and she been here playin' for hours and no one come ta' check on her, no one. I'm taking her home with us!"

"You crazy fool! You don't think her people lookin' fuh' her. Look at her. She looks like a little doll baby."

"I know. Can't I keep her honey?"

"I said let her go!"

The man knew his wife couldn't be reasoned with and lost control as anger consumed him. He jumped upon his wife, startling her as he wrestled the child from her grip and smacked her in the head. As soon as Baby Girl was free, she ran to the other end of the shelter to hide.

Meanwhile Fats had an exhausting day locating Ebony. After traveling to various locations on the south side he finally found her. When his high wore off he was at one of the bars on Fifth Street when he began to feel like he was forgetting something. It started gradually, the feeling, and increased as time wore on and his high subsided, since the alcohol smoothed out the cocaine, making it manageable. Fats had just finished gambling in the back room of the bar when his memory loss started annoying him. He felt he had forgotten something important. Fats wondered what it could be since he had already collected his money after eventually finding Ebony. When he went to Black's house in search of her, he was told she was there the previous evening but had gone, so he figured he might as well take care of some business and bought enough drugs to last a week. If it wasn't money or drugs he was missing, he figured it couldn't be that important, yet the feeling of loss saddened and overwhelmed him.

"What's wrong Fats?" the bartender asked with a smile for she liked him.

"I don't know. I keep thinkin' I'm fuh' gettin' somethin," Fats replied.

"Oh, I hate that feeling. One time I was rushing out the house and forgot my keys but I didn't realize it until I got to work. They weren't in my purse. I usually keep them in a section with a zipper. So, I got to worrying jus' like you are now cause, I didn't know if I left them at home. All sorts of thoughts ran through my mind. I started to retrace my steps and realized I never took them off the hook by the door, since I was rushing cause' I was runnin' late. You can do it too. Just retrace your steps. Do you have your car keys, house keys, and wallet?"

"Yeah, I got those."

"Retrace your steps and see what you find."

"When I left the house, I went to get Candy. She was late as usual and always complaining. We went ta' look for Ebony cause she didn't gimme' my money."

"Don't tell me she was holdin' out again."

"I know. Can you believe it? It's the second time dis' month but I doubt if there'll be a third cause' I put my foot in dat' ass real good."

"You can't trust someone like that. You better get another girl," the bartender said with a smile."

"Anyway, we couldn't go everywhere lookin' for her because I had my daughter wit' me, so I had to drop her off at Riverview……. Oh my God!"

"What's wrong?"

Fats couldn't bring himself to tell the bartender the truth for he could hardly believe it himself. He frantically jumped out of his chair, knocking the bar stool to the floor as he ran out the door without paying for his drinks.

"No, no, no, no," he kept mumbling to himself repeatedly while crying in the setting sun. As he ran to his mother's car, he couldn't believe he left his daughter in the park the entire day. He cursed himself for being stupid and negligent, and endangering the welfare of his child. He was afraid of himself, and his actions terrified him because they were unpredictable. If anyone would have told him that he would leave his child unattended, and then forget her, he would have bet his life that he wouldn't for he loved his daughter. Fats realized that he didn't understand his mind, it was a stranger to him, his thoughts were juvenile, selfish and dangerous.

Fats gripped the steering wheel tightly as he sped to Riverview Park. The thought of his daughter being alone and scared overwhelmed him, causing him to cry out, "Why!" As tears streamed down his face, he kept thinking what his mother would say if he returned without her. He would have to lie because her wrath would be harsh if she knew the truth. He would be looked upon unfavorably, because she was in his care, and Big Mama might even evict him from her mansion. Suddenly a car darted out into the intersection narrowly missing him. Luckily the driver slammed on the brakes and swerved from his path. Fats was at fault in the near collision. In his troubled state he ran a stop sign and almost crashed.

It was after eight o'clock in the evening when Fats reached the park. He couldn't imagine his daughter would still be at the shelter, still he had to go and search for her. He might be lucky and find her with someone who stayed around to wait with her until he returned, he hoped. He ran screaming her name as he approached the apparatus.

"Tinaaa! Tinaa where you at? Tinaaa! It's yo' daddy! I'm here baby! Where you at baby? Tina!"

There was no answer. The silence caused his knees to buckle and he stumbled about the dirt, terrified and alone as his heart ached. He clutched his chest for the pain was so severe he thought he was having a heart attack, and was filled with despair as he stood at the foot of the jungle gym.

"No! What have I done? Tinaaaa! Tina where you at!" He looked to the sky when he cried out and glimpsed at the bell tower and saw something move, he thought, so he focused on the object until a little head popped up and called out to him.

"Daddy I'm up here," she said and waved her arms. "See me daddy. See how high I am."

"I see ya' baby! I see you up there," he said and cried happily, and sank to the ground as his legs gave way, he collapsed from the stress that overwhelmed him. Being twenty, Fats never worried about anything. He was accustomed to people taking care of him. It was his choice to run the streets and try to emulate his mother, but it wasn't necessary. Big Mama would have been happy just to have him collect her money, and help around the mansion. She would never forgive him if Baby Girl was harmed due to his negligence, since it was unnecessary to leave her with anyone. Fats knew his mother would have been horrified to learn he left her alone, all day, unattended, so he cried and his heart beat joyfully now as she made her way to him. She was happy too, and relieved because her father had finally returned.

"Papa, you shoulda' seen me. I was playin' with the other kids and I climbed all the way to the top."

"That's my girl! I'm so happy to see you! I'm sorry I been gone for so long."

"Papa, wus' wrong? Why you cryin?"

"It's nuthin' my dear. Tears of joy das' all. Tears of joy," he said and scooped his little princess up into his arms and carried her away.

IV

GIMME' MY MONEY

    The Hendrix family left their home in Hilltop, on this cold and blustery day to travel to aunties house in north Dayton, Ohio, where the homes were bigger and more expensive, with manicured lawns and clean, tidy streets. I say north Dayton but it was only three blocks over on the north side of town. Hilltop was one of the safer sections in the Dayton Metropolitan Public houses, located on the south side of the city where low, income families lived. There were eleven sections in the public houses spread throughout the city, with Hilltop being the safest and Desoto Bass being the most dangerous, where liquor stores, gun stores, drugs, gambling, and prostitution permeated the area, spreading throughout, effecting every aspect of Desoto.
    Each section of the public houses had a gang that recruited all the children in that area, therefore, to grow up without joining a gang meant you had to avoid them every day, or fight them every day, or do a combination of both, in school and in the streets, every day. Some children were good in sports and could navigate between gang members, some of whom were their friends or classmates, and civilians. Their athletic skills made them popular and shielded them from the destruction of the gang, but it was a dangerous tightrope to balance and many children died even though they were not in a gang. They were shot and killed by accident while hanging out with their friends and family, struck by errant bullets intended for others. Some unfortunate children had parents who were gang members, so they had no choice in the matter, they were born into the gang. The only effective solution for safety was to leave the area, but many of the residents were poor and uneducated, preventing most of them from moving.
    The family walked their usual route through McCabe Park to get to the bus stop on McCall Street. McCabe Park was two acres of land that contained plush green lawns surrounded by a towering mixture of Pine and Oak trees, accompanied by dirt trails that took visitors to the playground, basketball court, restrooms and water fountains. They entered the park on McCabe Avenue and exited at

Home Avenue, walking the length of the park diagonally from base to tip since the park was shaped like a triangle. McCabe Park had a frightening aspect because it was dangerous to be there after dark when the gangs came out. There were male and female gangs with members ranging in age from twelve to adults, with the older members usually becoming the leaders that made the younger members do all sorts of terrible things under the cover of night, including robbery, assault, and rape, with rape being the most frequent atrocity.

The family stayed on the path but when they were about to pass the playground which contained a Shelter, Pam couldn't control herself. The urge to play on the apparatus was too strong, so she gave in to her need for fun and ran to the playground despite the protest from her mother.

"Come on now we ain't got no time for playin'!"

Pam ignored her mother and ran to her beloved; the horse that sat on a thick, metal, spring, which caused the rider to sway forward and backward. The horse was lavender with vibrant pink eyes that captivated Pam, putting her in a trance and not breaking the spell until she was worn, tired, and ready to let go because her hands were stinging from holding on so tight. It was her favorite ride. She loved it, the way it made her feel, so happy and free. Kids laughed at her because she stayed on the ride for long periods of time. They said that's why she's crazy, cause her brains were scrambled from swaying back and forth all day. Pam was unconcerned about their comments and would sway violently close to the ground, then stand up and lean forward, trying to make the horse stay in that position, only to have it spring back so forcefully that her head would snap back causing a whiplash effect. One time she lost her grip and fell backwards off the ride onto the soft sand, with her feet still on the pegs, causing the kids to laugh and point. Since then, Pam made sure not to act so wild on the horse.

"Come on or I'll leave yo' butt here!" her mother yelled and continued walking with Herby and Baby Girl.

The Shelter sat on a soft mixture of sand and dirt, designed with two, forest green towers that were connected by a thick, black, rubber foot bridge, which dipped in the middle and loosely swayed, causing the children to hold onto the white perpendicular bars that traveled the length of the bridge on both sides. The bars, which were made of chain and covered with white foam, connected to the towers and continued onto the platform of each tower, protecting the children from falling off. Some children cheated while crossing by crawling across the bridge, slowing down the other kids behind them, ignoring their protests. The first tower was shorter than the second. It had a round grey tubular plastic sliding board, and a conventional stairway covered with orange rubber, with a white hand rail that leads to its platform, under which, connected to its legs were three Styrofoam, beige, log shaped, blocks on spindles, decorated with letters and numbers. After crossing the foot bridge to the taller tower, the children were greeted by a yellow fun slide that was larger than the other slide, and curved circularly as it descended. A rope stairway connected to this tower. It had seven rungs with three boxes on each rung, and only the athletic kids attempted to climb it because their hands and feet would slip through the boxes if not placed precisely. A pole connected to this tower extended to the ground and the children used it to slide down when they played fireman. The horse with the spring sat near the tall tower. There was only one. Pam was enjoying her ride as she watched her family slowly disappear in the distance, but when she realized, they weren't going to wait for her she ran to their side.

   The weather was frosty so the children wore their wool coats. Herby sported a chocolate brown coat with a matching hat. It was his favorite coat and he always walked in rhythm when he wore it. His sisters wore matching grey coats. Ellen dressed them the same because she always wanted twins. When she was pregnant with Baby Girl, she hoped it was twins. In her third month of pregnancy her mother took her to the doctor after noticing her weight gain, for she didn't even know she was with child. She was seventeen, naïve, in love, new to sex, and happy her period had stopped, especially since it had just begun the year prior. She knew not to tell her mother, who had no idea she was having sex. When Ellen was given a Sweet Sixteen party at the church, her mother being a devout Christian, told her that she was a woman now but sex was saved for marriage, and she should abstain until then. Ellen's desire for twins and her disappointment upon finding out that she was not having them, resurfaced when Pam was born. Since she found out her second pregnancy was another girl and they were so near in age, her depression gradually subsided the closer she got to her due date, and when she gave birth, she had already decided to dress the girls alike. Pretending she had twins gave her the greatest joy and made her disregard her daughter's feelings, upsetting Baby Girl's entire adolescence. She was angry that her mother dressed them this way, after all, she was the oldest and felt she should have her own identity, and not be bound by fashion with her deceitful sister.

    They boarded the number nine bus at McCall Street and headed downtown where they would transfer to another bus at the corner of Third and Main, heading to north Dayton. The children boarded the bus first and Ellen only paid for herself. The driver frowned but didn't protest because he knew he was in a poor area and didn't want to start an argument, which might cause a delay. The children sat across from their mother in the middle of the bus next to the side door. They sat in two row seats with Pam and Herby sharing one seat and Baby Girl sitting alone behind them. Ellen could have sat next to her but since depression returned, she acted as if her children were strangers, showing them no love or affection, and only sat with them if she had to, but today the bus was fairly empty since it was after the morning rush, so she sat alone. The children would have all sat together, crammed into one seat, if not for Baby Girl. She was tired of her family too, and even though her siblings wanted her to sit with them she declined. She was happiest when she was away from them. Although she was only seven, she knew her mother was neglectful, and she hated the responsibility of caring for her siblings.

    Herby was happy because he had money, well, he called it money but it was only a few coins, six to be exact. He was three years old and liked coins instead of paper money since coins were shinny and came in different sizes, and had different faces on the front, with various pictures, designs, and words on the back. He couldn't read but he would caress the words and pictures on each coin with his little chubby fingers. He didn't know that paper money was worth more than coins and he didn't care, because he wasn't going to spend them anyway. He collected the coins and had his current collection for almost a week. First, he had two nickels, then three dimes, and now a quarter. It was his treasure and he treated it as such, hoarding it, and joyfully analyzing each piece, in secret, like a miser. He sat in the seat next to the window and quietly fingered the coins in his pocket until he discovered that one was missing. He knew the missing coin was a nickel without taking the coins out of his pocket, because he could feel them in his hand

and since they were different sizes this made detection easier. Herby wanted to be certain so he removed the coins, hunched over and stared into his palms while cuffing the coins with both hands as if he were praying. Pam stopped jumping in her seat long enough to ask him what he was doing. Herby slowly looked up with furious eyes and scornfully stared at Pam.

"What's wrong wit' you?" she asked.

"I know you got it!" he yelled.

"Got what, whatchu' got in yo' hands. You got money? Where you git' money from? Mommy.... Herby got money! You gave him money and I didn't git' nun! How you gonna' do dat? Tina... Tina... Tina! You got money too? You hear me talkin' to ya!"

"What are you screaming about. I don't have any money," Baby Girl replied.

"I don't believe you. Imma' look fo' myself!"

"You ain't gonna' do nothing. Now sit down and be quiet before I pop you."

Her remarks caused Ellen to smirk, unintentionally, because she sounded like an old lady scolding her child.

"I know you got it! You betta' give it back. You took my muunie!"

"I didn't take nuthin' you crazy!"

Pam was a thief but in this case she was innocent. Since she always stole things, she was the first to be held responsible when something was missing. She hated being blamed when she wasn't guilty, so her brother's accusation infuriated her.

"I ain't crazy! Gimme' my muunie! I ain't playin' wit' you! Give it here! I want my muunie, gimme' my muunie, where's my muunie!"

Herby was out of control, and screaming, and started hitting Pam.

"Get offa' me stupid. I didn't take nuthin," she said while hitting him back. This went on for quite a while as the bus traveled on its route toward downtown Dayton. Ellen ignored her children as they argued but Baby Girl became annoyed when they didn't stop. She was happy she chose not to sit with them and refused to intervene. If Ellen wasn't going to stop them from fighting, neither was she, no matter how much she wanted to. She was determined to make her mother care, and she knew if she stayed quiet her mother would have to act.

Herby was determined to get his nickel. He wasn't going to let his sister steal from him and get away with it. He turned in the seat so his back was facing the window, using the bus to support him, he started kicking his sister off the seat, but Pam was accustomed to fighting and wasn't afraid of a baby, so she held his legs and looked at her mother when Herby began screaming, but Ellen looked away, out the window, far off into the distance. Realizing her mother wasn't going to intervene, Pam sat on his legs, preventing him from kicking her again. As he struggled to free himself, he began to growl like a dog, and spit saliva from his mouth. This was intended to frighten Pam but she just laughed since she was a sociopath, and enjoyed causing people pain. Her laughter enraged Herby and even though he couldn't move his feet he began hitting the window with his hand. There were more passengers on the bus now, and they all looked with disgust at the children when they heard the sound Herby was making from hitting the glass.

"Whose kids are those? Those some badass kids right dare'. I'd whip dey' ass if it was me!"

There were two young men sitting in the back of the bus that were upset by the unwanted chaos. They were tired of the commotion and just wanted to travel in peace, but these were no ordinary men. They were gang members and wore black bandanas under their hats. One of the men spoke again, he was the slender of the two and sported a neatly trimmed mustache and beard.

"Where dey' momma at? Badass kids need ta' shut up!" the man yelled, and awoke Ellen from her trance. The man's voice was louder and more agitated now, forcing Ellen to focus her attention on what was happening. Gradually she emerged from her spell and realized Pam and Herby were fighting, but the passengers blocked her view so she could only yell her protest.

"Y'all betta' stop fighting. Pam! Herby! What y'all doin' over there?!" One lady moved to the side so Ellen could see her children.

"I can't take y'all nowhere. Pam get off yo' brutha!"

As soon as Pam moved and Herbys' legs were free, he started kicking her again.

"Momma Pam got my money! She took it! She stole it!" Herby yelled as he kicked his sister.

"No I didn't. You betta' stop lyin' on me boy!" Pam

screamed and retaliated by hitting her brother with force now. It was a complete brawl with no child backing down as passengers moved completely out of the way as if to say to Ellen, stop them from fighting.

"I know y'all betta' stop all dat' noise up dare, wit' yo' badass!" the slender gangster yelled. His comments prompted Ellen to act again because he made her nervous.

"I said stop all that fightin' now! Stop it! Pam let him go! Herby stop kicking her! Tina why ain't you sayin' nothing. You see dem' actin' up an you jus' let em."

Until then the passengers weren't aware that Baby Girl was with them.

"Damn, how many kids she got! That's why she can't take care of um'. I would beat dey' ass. All dey' need is a good whopping!" the gangster yelled, and some of the passengers nodded in agreement. All of a sudden Herby, already frustrated and angry, addressed the man directly.

"Mind yo' business mannnn! Ain't nobody talkin' ta' you!"

"Herby! Shut yo' mouth! Don't chu' talk ta' that man like dat!"

"But momma! Pam took my money and she won't give it back!"

"No I didn't!"

"Yes you did!"

"No I didn't!"

"You did so!"

"Just be quiet now, we'll talk about it later!"

"No! I want my muunie!"

"Whip his ass lady!" the slender man yelled, and his friend laughed.

"Mind yo' business man! Dis' ain't got nuthin' ta' do wit' you!" Herby shouted. He was in fighting mode now and didn't care who he was screaming at. Since he was only three, his happiness was shattered by the theft, and someone had to pay because he wasn't going to be the only one suffering.

Ellen was shocked by her son's outburst, and unequipped to handle the situation. Since her depression returned, she was unable to touch her children. She didn't hold their hands when they crossed the street, she crossed alone, in front of them while Baby Girl held her siblings' hands, instinctively playing the role of mother, with Pam on one side and Herby on the other since she knew to keep them separated if there was to be peace, but now she was tired of being dependable, and angry with her mother for being neglectful, so she refused to intervene. Ellen desperately looked to Baby Girl for help but she wouldn't make eye contact with her.

The gangsters wore black wool Peacoats with wide lapels, and two columns of onyx buttons that descended four rows, accompanied by two hand pockets near the chest and two more full sized pockets at the bottom, below the waist. The men had their lapels turned up around their necks, completing their essence of style. They wore high top Converse tennis shoes that were clean but not new, denim blue jeans, and carried knives, which was common among gang members because they never knew when they would come across a rival. The larger man was quiet even though he was agitated by the children. He thought the commotion was amusing, but his partner was a serious man and felt slighted by the boy. He felt the child wasn't giving him the proper respect since he was used to being feared, and if someone wasn't afraid of him, he'd pull his knife.

"I said stop all that noise and get off yo' sista!"

"Tell her to give me back my money!"

"Pam, give it back to him!"

"I didn't take nuthin! He lyin."

"You ain't got no damn money! What kind of money a little baby gonna' have!" the gangster yelled again.

"I told you ta' mind yo' business mannn!"

Herby responded like an adult, with a low voice, quite different from the high, pitched squeals he was making before, and he stopped kicking Pam as he stood in his seat, and looked to the rear of the bus to see the man.

"You ain't got nuthin' ta' do wit' dis' mannn!" he said with emphasis and body language, swiveling his head as he pointed his chubby little finger while moving his neck from side to side, like he observed Pam doing so many times before.

"So, mind yo' business cause ain't nobody, talkin' ta' you!" he screamed.

Now Pam opened her mouth wide, stunned by her brother's boldness, because she had always been the outspoken one when it came to addressing adults, even though she was only five. She hid her amazement with her hands, since she began to laugh when

Herby continued to mimic her as he swirled his head and neck from side to side, while rhythmically pointing to the back of the bus as he spoke, to emphasis his words.

"Ain't... no... body... talkin' ... ta'...you!"

"Ain't... no... body... talkin' ... ta'... you!"

"Ain't... no... body... talkin' ... ta'... you!" Herby chanted, as Ellen grew frantic when she saw the gangster try to move toward Herby, only to be held by his friend. I say held but it wasn't a hard restraint. When the slender, light brown man, took one step in Herby's direction, the larger, coffee complexioned gangster, placed his hand on the man's shoulder and that was all it took to stop him. This was because the larger man was really the one in charge. He would let his partner mouth off and put on a show but when it came to an unnecessary conflict, especially involving a child, he had to put a stop to it, but still he smiled for he was enjoying himself, and planned to tease his friend for letting a baby get the best of him. He knew he had to wait because if he teased him now his friend would truly fight to get to the boy.

"Herby! You shut yo' mouth right now! Y'all kids out here actin a fool embarrassing me like dis! I swear I can't take y'all nowhere!"

"You need to beat him!" the slender gangster responded with disgust. It was the first time he spoke to Ellen directly. She could see the anger in his eyes and was afraid, and he could see the fear in her eyes and grew bolder for this was a familiar site to him, one that he welcomed, her fear comforted him because all he knew was intimidation.

"Man, ain't nobody talkin' ta' you! I keep telling you ta' mind, yo' business! Shut yo' mouth right now! Shut up! Shut... yo'... mouth! Shut uuuup! Shuuuuuuut up! Herby chanted, annoying everyone, trying to drown out the angry gangster, unafraid because he knew the man wouldn't hit him, but he really didn't care if the man did, he was having a tantrum because he believed Pam stole from him and was getting away with it, which was too much for him to accept, it was also too much for his mother to tolerate and her fear took over, forcing her to jump to her feet and pull the cord for the bus to stop. Fortunately, the nearest stop was a block away.

"Tina...get them...we gettin' off dis' bus!"

"That's right...you betta' git' dem' kids outta' here fo' dey' git' dey' ass whopped!" the slender gangster yelled when he realized what was happening.

"But dis' ain't our stop! Why we gettin' off here! Mama... why we gettin' off here? Mama... you hear me mama? Mama...why we gettin' off here mama... mama!" Herby yelled. He couldn't understand that he was at fault for their early departure, but the slender light skinned gangster made sure he knew.

"Cuz' a yo' badass, you little baby!" the gangster yelled.

The whole bus laughed, including the driver, and the gangster's partner, who was relieved because he finally got to laugh heartily since he was suppressing it for most of the ride. Ellen was mortified. She didn't want everyone to know that this wasn't their stop. She just wanted to strangle Herby, quickly, snatching him and crushing his neck while watching his eyes pop out, but her thoughts of murder were not enough to end her son's tantrum.

Finally, the stop arrived and the passengers moved so the family could depart, as the slender gangster continued to yell that he would whip the kids. The family got off the bus at the corner of Lakeview and Summit Avenue, in front of Daymount West, which was a psychiatric hospital. Ellen just walked off the bus, to the surprise of everyone, leaving Baby Girl to gather her siblings and hold their hands. The three little children huddled closely, walking in stride, following their mother who was furious because they still had to travel some distance to get to aunties house. The slender gangster said what everyone on the bus was thinking.

"Damn, look at huh', she don't even want dem' kids...."

V

ELLEN KIDS ALWAYS STEALIN'

"Ellen kids always stealin'! I come into my bedroom and see that my favorite perfume is gone, and my silver necklace with the red stones is missing too. Little thieves took em' I know they did. I can't take it no mo! That's why I don't likes em' in my house. You gotta' watch them kids. Even the little one. I know he only three but I don't trust him either. They wasn't always this bad but now every time they come over sumthin's missing. Them damn kids! Ellen don't even watch em' She jus' let em' run wild. Now I only let em' in the house ta' use the bathroom. They can't come in my kitchen and they definitely can't go upstairs. They be sneakin' round'. You can't trust a sneak. I ain't bout' ta' be hidin' my thangs' in my own house jus' cause' them little devils come around either. I'll stop em' from comin' over before I do that. Imma' talk ta' Ellen. She betta' bring my thangs' back. I don't care if she is my sister, she won't be welcomed here. I'm surprised cause' Mama always tried ta' raise that girl right. Took her ta' church every Sunday, taught her right from wrong, kept a clean house, and always had food on the table. I don't know what happened cause' Ellen turned out terrible. She don't teach them kids nothing. Well, I'm not havin' it. They won't be comin' here if they can't act right!"

Aunt Mae was angry, and tired of being stolen from so she screamed and yelled her discontent as she walked around her bedroom looking to see if anything else was missing.

"I ain't bout' ta' be lockin' the door ta' my room. No sir. I never locked it before and I'm not startin' now. Especially not for some little thieves. My chilrens' know betta' than ta' come in my room so I'm not worried bout' dem'. Amanda! See if you missin' anything. I'm bout' ta' call Ellen and I wanna make sure we take a count of every thang' before I do."

Aunt Mae was forty, three, eighteen years older than her sister Ellen. She had a serious personality and she rarely smiled or joked with people. She was tall and had a sturdy build with a caramel complexion accompanying her short, black, afro. She had two children, her daughter, Amanda, was ten and her son Morris Jr. was eight. Mae was a hardworking woman, always having two jobs, but she really should have been a chef, cooking in her own restaurant, for her skills were superior. She could make everything including cakes and pies.

Mae expressed her joy of cooking by having the family barbecues and gatherings at her house. It was always a grand affair attended by relatives and friends, where she prepared all the food to the delight of everyone. Every Friday she would have a fish fry and sell dinners and whiskey. Her fish fries were accompanied by card games of Spades, and Pinochle, where the players gambled, and sometimes played until the early morn. Her favorite saying when yelling at the kids was, "Y'all get outta' my kitchen," or, "Ain't no playin' in here!"

Ellen was the youngest of her siblings and the rumor was, she wasn't their biological family, she wasn't blood, which made Mae less tolerant of her negligence. Mae believed her niece was innocent but still included her when she said, "Them kids be stealing," or "Ellen's kids always stealin' my thangs," and Baby Girl hated this. She hated being included amongst thieves, especially when she knew her sister Pam was the culprit. Aunt Mae knew her niece was intelligent, and always said that she was the only one in her family that had some sense, but she still included her when she condemned the children.

It began some time ago. Pam start stealing things when she was three, but Baby girl didn't realize it until a year ago when Pam turned four. She took her to the grocery store and was appalled when she returned home and Pam emptied her pockets filled with items she had stolen. She noticed when Pam stole something she would sit quietly next to her, that was Pam's tell, since Baby Girl never actually saw her steal anything, but she knew her sister was always running around getting into trouble, so to see her sit quietly was unusual, over time, after repeatedly doing this, it was obvious that Pam had stolen something, and Baby Girl would display anger in her expression when she stared at Pam. She would even try to get her sister to put it back. She would say, "I know you took something. You better put it back. You gonna' get us in trouble," but since she didn't know what her sister had stolen, she was at a disadvantage, because Pam would always lie and say she didn't take anything.

On this particular evening, the theft happened just before they departed. Pam noticed as they played in the backyard that her aunt was helping a friend carry some things to her car. She knew they would be leaving soon because Mae informed them that their mother was coming. The cousins played together the entire day. The children jumped rope, played hop scotch, and jacks, in front of the house on the sidewalk since they needed the concrete for these games. When they were bored and wanted to play something else, they ran to the backyard because it was large enough to play hide and seek, hula hoop, and tag.

Pam was subtle when she stopped playing with her cousins, saying she was tired. They ignored her as she casually walked along the edges of the yard, in increments, quietly making her way to the back door. She went unnoticed as she sat next to the door and soon disappeared inside the house when she turned the knob and found the door to be unlocked. She was smart enough to close the door behind her so no one would be curious and investigate. Once inside she stood in the kitchen and scanned the area, but there was nothing she wanted so she walked to the next room, passing the dining room which was off to the side, and into the living room where she happily took some coins that were left on one of the lamp tables. She looked around for other things to steal. She was bold because the house was occupied. She could hear women talking upstairs, and hid behind the drapes when they came down and went into the kitchen. Pam was undetected as she quietly stood behind the drapes, waiting for the women to leave, but they remained in the kitchen, talking and sipping drinks they made for themselves. She grew impatient and wanted to go upstairs to the bedrooms because she knew there was always something good to steal, so she peaked from behind the drapes to see if the women were looking in her direction, they were not, and didn't notice her as she crawled along the carpet. She stayed close to the wall, leaving the living room and entering the foyer that leads upstairs. Pam was small but knew how to make herself even smaller when she wanted to sneak around. She took her shoes off before ascending the stairs, to be as quiet as possible. Once at the top she heard the front door open. Her aunt returned from helping her friend and upon hearing voices in the kitchen she called out.

"Who's in my kitchen!"

"It's just us!" the women replied. Nicole and Barbra were

Mae's good friends and attended most of her cookouts.

"Oh, I thought those children were in my kitchen. They know not to come in here. You gotta' watch em,' mine are okay but those other three are trouble."

"Ellen's kids?"

"Yeah, you know it."

"Lord I don't know what's wrong with that child. She don't even take care of them kids."

"I know. I feel sorry for em' that's the only reason I let em' stay here all day while their mother's gone doing who knows what. She's on her way now ta' get em' cause I'm tired, and they can't spend the night no mo."

"Why? What happened?"

"Girl, every time they stay my things is missing. I had ta' put a stop to it."

"Oh no! Don't tell me they stealing. Them children so little. I can't believe they taking stuff already."

"I didn't believe it either, and I never seen em' take anything but when they leave, I notice stuff is missin', then I call Ellen and make her bring it back. That's how I know it's them. Sometimes Ellen brings back my stuff and sometimes she don't, cause you know them devils will lie and say they ain't take nothing."

"That's a shame. Them kids sure got a bad start in life. They gonna' need somebody."

"My brother Stanley helps her when he can. He says the only one got some sense is little Tina. That girl is something else. She like a grown little woman."

Pam was bold as she entered Mae's bedroom since she had been there before. She liked the little colorful bottles of perfume her aunt kept on the dresser and was careful not to spray them in order to remain undetected, because the scent would attract suspicion. It was a tall dresser and Pam used the foot stool at the end of the bed to stand on, so she could reach the perfume. She noticed a beige rectangular box in the rear of the dresser behind some of the bottles, next to the mirror. It was plain, but the clasp that closed the lid was a small, shiny, gold colored butterfly, and attracted her attention. She stretched her little arms pass the hair brushes, powders and perfumes to reach it. Pam smiled as she held the box with her little fingers, and her heart pounded from excitement as if she were opening a birthday present. She opened the box, running her fingers over the pretty butterfly clasp first, and her eyes brightened upon seeing the contents. Shiny trinkets greeted her gaze and caused her to giggle. She quickly snatched a necklace from the jewelry box. The silver chain adorned with red stones filled her with glee as she placed it into her pocket, along with a small, pyramid shaped, Jade colored perfume bottle. Now she was careless because she placed the jewelry box back on the dresser in a different location. Her theft caused her to be unconcerned with details now, and she hurriedly returned the foot stool to the end of the bed without smoothing the fabric to conceal her footprints, and tip toed out of the room. She heard someone quickly running up the stairs and figured it had to be one of the children. She was exposed as she stood in the hallway and had little time to hide.

"Who that going upstairs?!" Mae called out after hearing footsteps.

"It's me, mama!" Amanda replied, stopping her ascent to answer her mother, giving Pam just enough time to find a hiding place. She retreated back into the bedroom and hid behind the door as Amanda ran past, down the hallway, and into her room. Amanda wanted to give Herby, some coloring books to take home, so she rummaged through her things to find them.

On the second floor of Mae's house were three bedrooms, a bathroom and two large hall closets. Pam hid behind the open door and peaked through the crack to see Amanda leaving with the coloring books. She listened and only emerged from the room when she heard Amanda descend the stairs and walk towards the kitchen. She couldn't be caught upstairs and was afraid her aunt would hear her footsteps so she removed her shoes once again, crept down to the foyer and waited, unsure of what to do next. She couldn't leave the way she came, through the back door, so she decided to leave out the front door, which was open and only the screen door was closed. It was a thin aluminum door and the screen kept the flies and mosquitoes outside while letting in fresh air, cooling the house in the summer time. She was relieved to find the door unlocked and happily turned the knob and pushed the door open, but to her horror, there was a latch three feet above the knob that was fastened, keeping the door from opening completely, this kept people from entering from the outside. It was feeble security and only consisted of a metal hook that inserted into a metal loop fastened to the door frame, but it could only be unhooked from the inside. Pam pushed the door again and was terrified because this flimsy latch had her trapped since it was too high for her to reach. She was short so she stood on her toes with her arms fully extended but still couldn't reach the latch. She panicked because she believed she would soon be discovered. She thought of how embarrassing it would be, getting caught, and questioned, maybe even searched, or spanked. She would do anything to avoid detection, to avoid the feelings of shame and sadness it would cause. Her fear made her entire body tremble nervously. She quickly removed her shoes a third time and decided to jump up to hit the latch in hopes of knocking the hook free. She sat her shoes quietly on the wooden floor in the foyer a few feet from where she stood and jumped, hitting the latch, which moved, but not enough to unhook, making a clanging noise. The sound surprised her and she knew she couldn't avoid making noise if she wanted to free herself. She jumped again, hitting the latch once more to no avail. This time the sound was even louder but Pam was encouraged because she almost knocked the hook free. Then it happened, her knees began twitching, her legs became numb, she was unable to stand and collapsed to the floor. She was terrified because she couldn't move her body from below her waist. She was in physical pain and mental anguish caused by the stress of being trapped. Her legs were stinging, and tingling like she was being pricked with pins and needles. It would be too embarrassing to be caught like this, sprawled on the floor with stolen goods in her pockets so she pressed her palms together like she had seen her grandmother do. She closed her eyes and prayed to God to help her escape. It was a selfish prayer for she was selfish, afraid, and her fear caused her to cry out to the Lord for forgiveness. Even though she lacked the words, since she never prayed before, she believed that people only prayed to ask for something, and all she could think to do was beg.

"Please, please, please, please, please, please, please, help me Jesus," she mumbled over and over again. "Help me Lord. Please, please, please, help me God."

She didn't understand that you can't ask God to help you do something evil, but since she was only five, and malicious, she only cared about herself. As she lay on the floor, she heard the women leaving the house through the back door and believed her prayers were answered. This belief gave her the strength to stand on her wobbly legs. When she was upright, Pam scanned the foyer and saw the various potted plants assembled. Aunt Mae had embedded a stick in the soil next to each plant, and tied them to it, to strengthen them, so the young plants would grow straight and tall. Pam was a clever child but she used her intelligence to lie, steal, and hurt people. She figured she could use one of the sticks to knock the latch free. She stumbled over to a plant and untied the stick, and removed it from the pot causing the plant to immediately leaned to one side, but she was unconcerned and only thought about her escape. It was easier now as she used the stick to flick the latch free. It took several tries but she didn't care about the noise because the women had gone. On her fourth attempt she flicked the latch from the hook, swung the door open and left the house, stumbling down the steps, still holding the stick as the children ran to the front of the house and confronted her.

"Where were you? We were looking for you," Amanda asked.

"I was up here."

"No you wasn't. We came up here already."

"When you came up here that's when I went to the backyard, y'all was gone so I came back to the front. We was jus' missin' each other."

"You lyin' You always lyin' I know you was doin' something."

"I ain't lyin' I wasn't doin' nuthin."

"What's that stick for?"

"Nuthin' Jus' poking stuff with it, das' all."

"Yeah right. Put it down and stay with us. I gotta' keep my eyes on you. Yo' mama coming soon and I don't wanna have to look for you when she git' here." Amanda was suspicious because Pam had stolen before. The children returned to the backyard and Pam sat quietly next to Baby Girl.

"Y'all don't wanna play anymore?" Morris Jr. asked.

"I'm tired, besides mama on her way," Baby Girl replied, and looked at her sister who wouldn't make eye contact with her, and she immediately knew that Pam had stolen something because she had seen her act this way before. After stealing, Pam would silently sit or stand next to her as if she were innocent and virtuous.

Ellen traveled by bus to Mae's house, but sometimes Mae's husband, Morris Sr., would give them a ride home in his 1970 Buick

Regal. The car was midnight black and built like a rocket, with a long hood that shot out like a canon, like the barrel of a Colt 45 hand gun, because it was designed for speed and racing. The hood had a double white stripe down the center, and a glossy silver, rectangular, grill adorned the front of the car, accompanied by four headlights, two on each side of the grill. The front of the car was pointed, surrounded by the bumper which was made of thick, heavy, aluminum. The rear of the car was short with a small trunk and fender that was less imposing than the front, but still sturdy and secure. It was a two, door vehicle and some people would enhance the cars' natural design to convert the automobile to a race car by putting an air vent on the hood, and large, slick tires on the rear of the car while installing a more powerful engine, to propel the vehicle as fast as possible in a quarter of a mile distance.

    The Buick Regal was strong, fast, and sturdy as it barreled down the highway returning Ellen and the children home. The thought of Pam's theft occupied Baby Girl's mind. She was nervous and knew by her sister's actions and demeanor that she had stolen something. Now she was depressed because she didn't want to be labeled a thief, and included in the crime just because they were siblings. Pam sat quietly as Herby bounced around in the back seat of the car. He enjoyed the ride and was happy whenever he got a chance to be in the car. Normally Pam would jump along with him while her sister tried to calm them, and tell them to behave, but not this evening. Pam was unaware that she acted differently when she stole something and Baby Girl wasn't about to tell her.

    Once home the children resumed their regular activities and soon were nestled comfortably in bed with no arguments, since they were tired from playing all day at their aunt's house. All the children slept in the same room even though there were two bedrooms. Herby and Candace had their own room but didn't use it because it was always cold and their mother feared the room was haunted. Baby Girl was relaxed since forgetting about her sister's theft, falling into a deep sleep she didn't hear her mother burst into the room and assault Pam. She only awoke when Herby jumped on her bed as the onslaught began, and witnessed her mother screaming at Pam as she beat her, shocking Pam from sleep with a flurry of slaps, continuing to strike the terrified, half awakened child until she jumped out of bed screaming, and ran into the edge of the opened door, sending her crashing to the floor in pain.

"That's good for your ass! That's what you get for always stealin!" yelled Ellen. She was startled at how fast her daughter hurdled from the bed as if she were possessed by the devil, or evil spirits. She jerked her head around and glared at Herby and Baby Girl who were crouched in a corner on the bed. With eyes squinted, and jaw clinched, Ellen frowned and showed her teeth, frightening her children. She didn't recognize them. In her fit of rage her mind, already weakened by depression, caused them to become strangers to her. Baby Girl saw the anger and confusion in her mother's eyes and was afraid as she held her brother.

"Mama, it was Pam. We didn't take nothing!" she yelled as Pam lay on the floor crying. Ellen stood over her, breathing heavy from beating her, while shifting her menacing gaze to each child.

"I know you didn't take nuthin' but you supposed ta' watch yo' sista' and make sure she behave," she snarled.

"But I tried. Pam always running around and hiding. She sneaky Ma. I can't watch her all the time."

"Well you betta' try harder. I'm tired of Mae calling me cause y'all stealin' her stuff."

"But I told you it wasn't me! I didn't take anything!"

"It don't matter. If you all together then you all guilty. Don't matter who done the taking, that's just the way it is. Pretty soon I won't be able to take y'all nowhere, cause' people don't want no thieves in their house."

Ellen was unaware of the mental pain and anguish she was causing her oldest child. She didn't know that her hurtful words sliced deeply into her daughter's heart, especially calling her first born a thief, and including her in the crime when she knew the child was innocent, when she knew Baby Girl was an angel disguised as a child, and she depended on the little woman, unfairly, to care for her siblings.

"It's not fair. You can't blame me if she sneaks around and steals something."

"Well Tina, that's the way it is, so you better get used to it, or stay away from her."

But Ellen knew there was no possibility of the sisters being apart because she always made sure Baby Girl was the guardian. The only time she had to herself was when she went to school. School was her solace and she thrived there, away from her depressed and neglectful mother, away from the needs of her siblings, she could finally think about herself. Her feelings mattered to her teacher, and her good deeds were celebrated and encouraged. Ellen knew Baby Girl was a capable caregiver because she witnessed it for herself, and enhanced it by doing less. She was unconcerned about her daughter's feelings for she was selfish and miserable since their father abandoned them. So, Baby Girl was filled with sorrow as she held Herby, and wished her family was educated and loving. She wished Pam wasn't a thief, and feared her mother was right in saying she had to leave her sister if she wanted to remain innocent.

Since she was too young, she didn't understand that someone could be convicted of a crime just by being with a criminal during the act, even if the person was unaware of the crime they still could be charged as an accessory; Ellen knew this, and though she was neglectful, her motherly instincts of protection wanted Baby Girl to realize that she could be arrested when she gets older, if Pam stole around her.

"Mama I don't wanna watch them no more. Can't you do it. I'm tired of taking care of them, you supposed to do that."

Her sorrow made her speak bluntly. She was tired, stressed, and wanted to be free of responsibility. She only wanted to care for herself and wished she could leave home. Her words penetrated her mother's anger and caused her to stomp out of the room, stepping over Pam as she left. Only the children remained now, in a frazzled state since the assault, unable to sleep they all cuddled on one bed, as Baby Girl told them happy tales of how their future would be if they did well in school, and were virtuous.

VI

THE BULLY

It was a cool September morning in Dayton, Ohio, and the sisters were slowly struggling uphill as they walked to Wogaman Elementary School. It was the shortest way. If they walked in the other direction, it would take them around the hill, which was a much longer route. As Baby Girl pulled her sister along, she was determined to take her to school today because when they left home her mother didn't even bother to awaken. Today, after waking her siblings and getting them dressed and feeding them, she had to sit her one, year old sister on her mother's bed, for she knew her mother would at least make sure she lived. She figured her three, year old brother would be fine until she returned, so she left him with some coloring books, a juice, and a sandwich. She was compelled to be the guardian today, therefore, failing to take her sister to school would have made her feel like her mother, whom she currently despised.

She was persistent and determined as she grabbed Pam's hand and pulled her along. Usually, she would walk in front and let her linger behind, but since Pam started lingering behind and returning home, she had to hold her hand and pull her along. She thought nothing about doing this, but today Pam was resisting and whining,

"Lemme' go, lemme' go..."

Pam's whining was annoying Baby Girl and she grew frustrated as she dragged her sister along, since she loved school, she was angry Pam didn't want to attend. She should have let her sister leave, but she couldn't because her anger controlled her now, and made her forget about her own happiness. Anger made her heart race and contorted her face as rage surged through her veins forcing her to scream,

"Come on ! Let's go now, I ain't gonna' be late cause a you! Come on now!"

Other children walked by them and laughed as they went up the hill on their daily trek to school, which was about a half miles journey. Pam yanked her hand away and tried to retreat, but Baby

Girl caught hold of the hood from Pam's red jacket, and dragged her up the hill.

"Lemme' go, let go you hurtin' me. Let go, lemme' go you hurtin' me. Let go, let go, let go, let go you hurtin' me, lemme' go, let go uh me!" Pam yelled and cried, she stomped her feet and flung herself onto the pavement. That was it. That was all Baby Girl could take. Her rage consumed her and she snapped as she repeatedly smacked her sister on her back and legs. Some older girls were walking by now and protested her treatment of Pam, and she screamed at them too,

"Mind your business!"

"No, you let her go. Don't hit yo' sista' like dat!"

Pam enjoyed this since she wasn't really hurt. She was just putting on a show so her sister would let her go. There was one child in particular who complained the most out of the group. She was a sixth grader named Jill. Baby Girl was in second grade and Pam was in first. She thought Jill was cool and saw her in their complex before. Jill was a tomboy and Baby Girl liked this. She admired how Jill walked with a bop, like a boy, with one blue jeans leg rolled up her calf. Jill was hard and she wanted to hang with her, but anger has a way of controlling people, so she wasn't able to stop herself from hitting her sister.

"I said get off her!" yelled Jill and pushed Baby Girl so hard that she fell to the ground.

"Why you do that?!" she exclaimed and jumped up. She was surprised, but her anger returned when she looked at Pam and saw a trace of glee in her eyes. She charged Jill, swinging wildly, repeatedly punching her as Jill helped Pam stand, then she turned around and pushed Baby Girl again. She stumbled back but didn't fall as Jill stood between the sisters. Her body shook from the rage that exploded in her stomach, caused by the taunting faces and hand jesters Pam was making behind Jill's back. Jill was a big, heavy set, onyx complexioned twelve, year old, and had a reputation for beating kids, so Baby Girl wasn't surprised when Jill charged her and knocked her down again. Pam smiled out right now, and even giggled as her sister struggled to her feet.

"Stop pushing me! I ain't messing with you. This between me and my sista!"

A small group of kids had gathered now because children love to see a fight. This made Jill happy since she knew her victim wasn't a threat and could easily be beaten. She was pleased because her reputation would grow as she conquered another opponent, even if it was only a second grader.

"No, you wanna' hit on yo' sista! You just pickin' on her!"

"Leave me alone. I gotta' take her to school!"

"You ain't gotta' take her, you ain't her mama, she'll go if you stop pullin' and hittin' on her!"

"No she won't, I gotta' take her so leave me alone!"

She tried to run past Jill to get to Pam, but Jill was too quick and pushed her to the side, then she punched and kicked her to the ground. She was overwhelmed and didn't want to fight anymore, but Jill was excited now and enjoyed the attention from the other kids as they chanted.

"Fight! Fight! Fight!"

Now, Pam was no longer smiling because she looked at her sister's demeanor and knew the situation was dire. She could see Jill's last assault hurt her.

"I don't wanna' fight, leave me alone!" Baby Girl yelled, then rolled onto her stomach, and attempted to stand but Jill grabbed her legs and dragged her along the ground, dirtying her coat. Jill dragged her about ten feet before she let her go, and rose her arms in victory to the cheers from the other kids. She was humiliated, dirty, and embarrassed as she struggled to stand amongst the laughter of the crowd. The kids pointed and laughed at her so much that her fury returned, and engulfed her fear, and caused her to charge Jill once again, taking her by surprise this time and almost knocking her down, but Jill stumbled, then regained her composure. The children responded with amazement…

"Ohhhh!" they exclaimed.

Pam could see the surprise in Jill's face turn to anger. Jill was willing to end the fight when her opponent was on the ground, but now that she had stood up and attacked her again, she felt disrespected and decided to make an example of her. Jill hadn't been fighting hard, but this time she punched her victim in the stomach with all her might, sending her crumpling to the ground. As she knelt defenseless, holding her stomach, moaning, Jill was about to kick her when Pam jumped on her back and fastened her forearm around her neck like she had seen the wrestlers do on television, and pulled tight. Pam was heavy for her age and used her weight to pull Jill to the ground as she choked her. She didn't let go until Jill stopped struggling. When she did release her, Jill coughed and gasped for air. Pam helped her sister to her feet as the crowd of children yelled and screamed with excitement at what they had witnessed. The girls were not amused and retreated down the hill towards home. It was no use trying to go to school now since Baby Girl was dirty and had to change her clothes. She was in no mood to learn after such a humiliating defeat. Pam was just happy to be returning home since she never wanted to go to school in the first place. Jill was distraught as she regained her composure, and felt betrayed by the very person she was trying to help. She was determined to get the sisters because they jumped her, which was the ultimate betrayal to a bully, and Jill knew her reputation would be tarnished because of this. How could she live with such an embarrassing defeat, at the hands of two babies? Her friends and fellow students would mock her, which was too much for her to accept. She was driven by the thirst for revenge as she made her way to school to release her aggression on some unsuspecting children.

  Herby was happy to see his sisters return home so soon. He was only three but he knew something was wrong because the girls were breathing hard from running most of the way.

  "What's duh madda' Tee Tee?!" he exclaimed, excitedly looking at his sisters with amazement and glee. Baby Girl's nickname was Tee Tee. Herby saw the dirt and grass stains on her clothes, and noticed the rip in Pam's sweater, and the scrapes on her arms.

  "What happen, y'all been fightin?"

  "Yeah, we got her good, right Tee Tee. You see me choke her like dat'. I had ta' do it cause' you was gettin' yo' butt whopped."

  Baby Girl didn't answer. She was too upset to speak because she really wanted to go to school today. It was Friday and her favorite teacher, Mrs. Wells, always gave toys to her smartest students on Friday. She would have her top five pupils sit together as she quizzed them on reading and math. Baby Girl wanted to display her knowledge and would often be the only girl at the table. The boys would protest her being selected because she always got a toy. This made her competitive and encouraged her to embrace any academic challenge.

  After she calmed down, she went about her day as if she

had gone to school, beginning her after school routine. First, she retrieved her infant sister from her mothers' room. As soon as Candace saw her, she squealed with excitement, while drooling and giggling. Baby girl lifted her off the bed and carried her on her hip as she returned to the kitchen.

"After I get cleaned up, we gonna' have school today, so get your stuff and meet me in the classroom," she said to Herby and Pam.

She used Herby and Candace's room for her classroom since they didn't sleep there. Herby happily retrieved his pencils and notebooks because he liked playing school, and Pam didn't mind because it was too early for her to watch soap operas like she usually did when she stayed home. In the room there were three little chairs, a table, a bed and crib. There was also a drawing easel that she used for her blackboard to display her lesson plan. Baby Girl felt important when she taught her siblings, and mimicked Mrs. Wells, whom she believed was a good teacher.

By Monday she felt energized and was surprised as Pam walked a few steps ahead of her, casually talking about a teacher that she hated and felt was picking on her. She usually had to pull her sister along but today was a welcomed change. She wished their mother wasn't sick and unable to take them to school. She was incapable of leaving the house now, but Baby Girl remembered when she was loving. She remembered holding her mothers' hand as she carefully escorted her to the steps of the school. She remembered feeling safe, confident, and loved, but since their father left their mother gradually stopped caring, and all of her feelings for anyone, or anything were gone, replaced by depression. She knew her mother was unable to help them mentally, or physically, and it saddened her. Since she had experienced her mothers' loving side, she focused on that, and transformed herself like an actress playing the part of a responsible parent.

The girls usually arrived to school late. All of the children were in their classrooms when the bell rung but the sisters were just appearing. This was their customary time and the teachers never marked them tardy. Entering Baby Girl's classroom was like being transported to little people land, with all the small desks, and chairs arranged. Everything was miniature and painted in bright colors, except for the teacher's desk. All the children were sitting on the floor in a circle when Baby Girl hung up her coat and joined them.

The kids were busy writing the letters of the alphabet and she sat down amongst them, unaware of the presence of Jill's sister Melanie, who sat across from her, angrily staring. At first all was well, but when Melanie's menacing stare went unnoticed, she began to taunt her classmate.

"My sista' gonna' get you...." she seethed.

Baby Girl looked up, surprised, for she was immersed in her school work and didn't realize Melanie was speaking to her until she repeated the taunt for the third time.

"My sista' gonna' get you..."

Melanie was the complete opposite of her older sister. She had a yellow complexion with mahogany freckles while Jill's complexion was dark, the result of having a different father. Where Jill was hard and tough, Melanie was soft and feminine, a girly girl, the kind Baby Girl hated. She wore dresses and pretty ribbons in her hair. Baby girl knew Melanie wasn't a fighter and wanted to make peace so she decided to ignore her taunts, but Melanie continued until other classmates became curious and started asking questions.

"What happened? Why she sayin' dat' to you?" they asked. Now she was unable to concentrate on her class work. She sat with her legs crossed on the floor amongst the children feeling alone, melancholy, with her chin in the palms of her hands, unable to stop the taunts and not wanting to hit her.

After school on the walk home Pam seemed excited.

"You ready Tee Tee?" she asked.

"Ready for what?"

"Jill gonna' fight you. I heard the kids sayin' it in school."

"What they say?"

"They say Jill gonna' fight you after school."

"No she not, anyway, I don't wanna' fight."

"Don't matter. You betta' get ready cause she beat you good last time."

Baby Girl was worried as they walked up the hill toward home. Melanie's words echoed in her mind and she understood her threat to be real. The hill stood between the school and their home. It was not a sharp climb but a steady incline that rose about a quarter of a mile to the summit. The distance to its peak was farther when they walked home and the sisters could see children gathering as they approached. Her heart began to race now as she saw Jill emerge from the crowd. She felt a tug on her sleeve as Pam clasped her arm.

"I told you..." Pam whined. "There's Jill, I told you she was gonna' fight you. You betta' get ready," Pam said as she took Baby Girls' book pack from her shoulder.

"Now, we gonna' do just like before. You fight her and if you start losin' I'll jump on her, okay."

"Gimme' my stuff. I'm not gonna' fight her, you'll see, just keep walkin."

As the sisters approached, Jill made a fist and started punching her hand.

"Come on babies. Come and get your whooping. Come on little cry, babies. Little stinkin' babies, you gonna' get it now!"

There were more kids this time, mostly second and third graders who jumped and screamed hysterically, anticipating the battle. Word of the fight spread through the cafeteria amongst the students at lunch time, so the children assembled into various groups as they ascended the hill. Schoolmates wrestled and scampered along as they laughed and whistled happily. A few of the children mimicked Jill behind her back, copying her hand jesters as she taunted the sisters who were slowly approaching, with Baby Girl walking ahead of Pam. Jill couldn't wait for them to reach her and ran down to confront them to the delight of the crowd,

" Ohhhhh!" the children exclaimed, and ran behind Jill to get a closer view.

"I don't wanna' fight!" Baby Girl yelled and held her hands up to block Jill's punches. Pam jumped back in amazement at how quickly Jill assaulted her sister, who then grabbed Jill by the waist. It was easy for her because she was short and slipped under Jill's arms by crouching down and running forward. Now, Jill was unable to effectively punch her and had to settle for pulling her hair, forcing her head back, and shoving her forearm under Baby Girls' chin to pry her loose, but she held on tight even though her neck had been forced back dangerously far. Pam decided this was the perfect time to attack and jumped on Jill, knocking them all to the ground. They landed in a pile with Baby Girl on the bottom, Jill on top of her and Pam on top of Jill. The crowd of children surrounded them, closing their circle of bodies and moving closer as the girls wrestled in the grass. Jill was the first to squirm free and stumbled to her feet, then kicked Baby Girl. It was a hard kick and caused her to cry out in pain as she held her stomach and curled into a ball. Next, Jill turned to Pam who was standing now, pushed her to the ground, wanting to keep the sisters close she dragged her on the grass and lay them together. The children especially liked the dragging part and cheered because it was the same thing Jill did to Baby Girl before. Now Jill took her time and methodically inflicted pain on both girls by stepping on various parts of their bodies. She especially liked standing on Pam's back, feeling Pam wiggle under her feet amused Jill, and she gradually began to feel satisfied with her conquest. Jill got off Pam and went to stand on Baby Girl, who anticipated the move and rolled out of the way. Jill tried to kick her but Pam held her foot causing Jill to trip. As Jill tumbled to the ground Pam stepped on her ankle and kicked her in the butt with all of her might. Jill moaned in pain as the crowd roared. The children were secretly rooting for the sisters because many of them had been bullied by Jill, and now they were delighted to see their bully disabled on the ground.

"Come on Tee Tee! Let's go!" Pam shouted and helped her sister stand. The sisters ran home as some of their classmates emerged from the crowd and ran along side of them, joyfully cheering and clapping.

The next day the walk to school was customary with Pam lingering behind, dragging her feet, then stopping to tie her shoe. Baby Girl was used to this and was silent as her sister lingered farther and farther behind. Finally, Pam stopped walking and watched as her sister grew smaller in the distance, disappearing from her view. She smiled because she didn't want to go to school and knew her sister was too far ahead to run back and get her, so she turned around and headed home, joyfully skipping along the way.

During school, Baby Girl's classmates were filled with curiosity and still excited about the fight they witnessed the day before. The ones that saw the fight questioned her about its origin and the ones that missed it were disappointed and briefed from their friends about the details. They kept asking if she was going to fight again. The inquiry continued during the morning session but waned at recess. The afternoon session was normal with Baby Girl happily immersed in her class work, but as school drew to a close the curiosity of the children resumed, so she decided to stay behind awhile and let the other kids walk ahead. She waited about fifteen minutes before departing and didn't see the crowd that gathered the day before. She was less guarded now as she ascended the hill, reached the summit and began her decent towards home. Her thoughts were occupied with food since she was hungry. She was looking forward to making a grilled cheese sandwich and holding Candace, who loved her unconditionally, and would always greet her with wide eyes, a bright smile and outstretched arms, but her attention was abruptly halted with a shove from behind. It was Jill and she was still angry and thirsty for revenge.

"Thought I forgot about you, huh!" Jill shoved her again as she kept walking, trying to avoid the altercation.

"Leave me alone!"

"You think Imma' let you kick me like dat!" she shoved her once more.

"I didn't kick you that was Pam!"

"You think I care. Where is that little pig anyway. Imma' get you both!" she shoved her again but this time Baby Girl swung around and hit Jill hard with her book bag. She tried to hit her again but Jill grabbed the bag, wrestled it from her and threw it to the ground.

"Oh, you wanna' hit me with stuff, huh!"

"You hit me first, now gimme' my bag I gotta' go home."

"You ain't goin' nowhere," Jill said, and kicked the back pack out of reach. Baby Girl was upset now and threw a flurry of punches most of which were blocked by Jill.

"You finished now little baby, that's all you got?" Jill laughed, lowered her shoulder, and rammed her like a linebacker on a football team, with such force it knocked her victim back three feet, sending her crashing to the ground, landing violently, causing her head to snap back. Baby Girl was shocked now and truly afraid because she knew she was no match for Jill, who now smiled at her accomplishment, seeing her victim sprawled on the grass she decided to humiliate Baby Girl and sat on her chest. Jill enjoyed inflicting pain, and her thirst for revenge waned with each passing moment as she watched her victim struggle, and soon Jill's anger subsided, all that was left was folly, as she amused herself by playfully slapping Baby Girl's face.

"Get off me, get off me, you betta' get offa' me, get off me!"

"Whatchu' gonna' do now, huh', you can't do nuthin' now, cry baby! Whatchu' gonna' do? You gonna' cry, huh', little baby!

I know you wanna' cry. Come on, lemme' see ya' cry little baby!"

"Hey, get offa' that little girl! You should be ashamed uh yo' self messin' wit' that chil'. You know you too big to be doin' that. Why don't you pick on someone your own age!"

A lady protested as she approached the girls, to their surprise, since Jill was too busy humiliating her prey to notice the woman before, but now she grew nervous because the woman was a big, heavy, set lady, and seemed determined as she grabbed Jill and pulled her off Baby Girl, who quickly retrieved her school bag and ran down the hill towards home. In the distance she could hear Jill's taunts and knew their conflict wasn't over.

"You betta' run!" Jill shouted. "You betta' run little cry baby! You ugly little pig! Imma' get you, you ugly stinkin' pig! You betta' run!"

The next day as she traveled to school, she was aware of her dilemma. She knew to expect a fight if she encountered Jill, she knew it couldn't be avoided even if she tried to walk way because Jill was determined, but it wasn't meant to be and she was relieved. She didn't know that Jill had been suspended as a result of cursing a teacher. All she knew was that Jill didn't appear after school. Baby Girl looked behind, in intervals, as she walked home, cautiously scanning her route from one side to the other, but there was no surprise attack from her enemy.

With each passing day, school life returned to normal and brought her joy once again. Soon she stopped constantly thinking about Jill, and gradually, only thought about her tormentor in passing, as her fears were replaced by reading, math and spelling. Her confidence returned as she successfully answered every question and completed all of her assignments. She knew her strength lie in her ability to learn but she wondered how this would help her defeat, Jill. She wondered how intelligence could defeat physical strength. She knew her persecutor couldn't be reasoned with, and she had no desire or money to bribe her. Before their conflict she admired Jill and wanted to hang with her, thinking she was cool, admiring the boyish way she carried herself, but now there could be no friendship since Jill hated her. She wished she could explain that it was all a misunderstanding, but she couldn't find the words, and realized that mentally, her enemy was like Pam and wouldn't accept an apology. Baby Girl recognized the meanness, it was familiar to her from dealing with her sister. She realized that Jill, like Pam, enjoyed hurting people and making them cry. She knew she couldn't reason with a person like that, if anything, reasoning might make things worse because Jill might interpret it as a sign of weakness.

Baby Girl was in high spirits when she attended class and enjoyed the daily drama that unfolded there. It was a month into the semester, and with twenty, seven kids in the room with various personalities, something unexpected seemed to occur daily. Reading was one of her favorite activities, therefore, when Mrs. Wells informed the class that everyone would take turns reading aloud, she grew excited and wanted to show the teacher her reading skills. Each child read a passage from the book, "The Adventures of Frog and Toad." When it was her turn, she read quickly and smoothly, carefully pronouncing each word without any mistakes. When she finished, she looked up and was greeted with a smile because Mrs. Wells was pleased when her students were learning.

Next the teacher called on Tyrone to read, causing the students to grumble, because they knew he was a terrible reader and always retarded the story. Tyrone was a special child. He was tall, dark, thin and mean. He wasn't a bully because he wouldn't start trouble, but she noticed certain peculiar traits he possessed. Tyrone would hit his classmates, hard, if they messed with him, and tell them the reason why. If you touched him, he would hit you and yell in a deep voice, "Don't touch me!" If you touched his belongings, he would hit you and yell, "Don't touch my stuff!" If you cut in front of him on the pencil sharpener line, he would hit you too. Every infraction was accompanied by a punch and an explanation.

As Tyrone struggled to read, she smiled because she liked being the best at everything and knew he was no competition. Tyrone stammered and stumbled through sentences, slowly reading in a monotone voice, awkwardly stopping at each period for far too long, making the class think he would not proceed, and when he did proceed, he was greeted by a chorus of moans. Suddenly he hit a roadblock and couldn't continue. The word he couldn't pronounce was "favorite," and each time he tried, he looked up from the book to the teacher for approval.

"Fa, fa, family?" he guessed.

"No, sound it out."

"Fa, faa, faav, faav, finally?"

"No, there's an 'O'. Make the 'O' sound."

"Ooo, ooo, ooo."

"Now, sound it out."

"Faa, faavo, faaavoo. Faaavooot"

"Favorite," another student called out.

"Don't tell me! It's my turn, don't tell me the word! I'm readin!"

"Settle down Tyrone, it's alright, you can continue, take your time you'll get it."

That's what Baby Girl liked about Mrs. Wells. She was a patient and kind teacher who encouraged all her students. Sometimes, like today, she would take extra time if a child was having trouble, but in order to move things along and keep her pupils from becoming restless, Mrs. Wells helped Tyrone.

"The word is favorite. Sound it out for me."

"Yes Mrs. Wells. Favorite, fa-vo-rite." Tyrone seemed relieved that she told him the word and continued to read the remainder of the paragraph. He slowly proceeded but as soon as he was about to reach the end, he encountered the word again, and still couldn't pronounce it. That's when Baby Girl realized something was wrong with him. Tyrone had more than anger management problems. He seemed genuinely slow, mentally. She realized that his outburst were really tantrums a baby would have, but since he was eight years old, his actions were more destructive.

"Fa, faa, faavooo…"

"Favorite, you, big, dummy!" yelled Lewis, who was a bully, and not afraid of anyone. His response caused the rest of the class to roar with laughter.

"Don't tell me! Don't tell me da' word! I'm readin' now! It's my turn now!" Tyrone yelled, and his hands started to nervously shake. Lewis mimicked Tyrone's words but said them in a baby voice, causing the class to laugh once again. Baby Girl was surprised when Tyrone threw his book at Lewis. Then Tyrone jumped up, lifted his chair and attempted to throw it too, but Mrs. Wells quickly intervened. Baby Girl marveled at the chaos that exploded, and sat riveted as the rest of the students jumped from their seats too, and began running around. The teacher wrestled the chair from Tyrone, placed it on the floor, and forcefully sat him on it.

"Now don't move! Everyone else, take your seats! Hurry now. Stop running and take your seats! Let's go!" she yelled, while clapping her hands and chasing after various pupils as if they were chickens on a farm. After gathering them together and restoring order, she focused on Tyrone again.

"Leave the classroom now! Go to the principal's office!"

"No!" Tyrone yelled as he folded his arms, slumped in his chair and pouted.

"I said go, now!"

"Nooo!" he yelled, holding onto the bottom of his chair as if to say, I will not be moved.

"I don't have time for this. You sit quietly and read to yourself and don't interrupt the class."

"Tell em' stop botherin' me!"

"No one is bothering you. Now just sit there and behave!"

She couldn't believe it. She was astonished at how the teacher restored order. She had never seen a teacher compromise with a student before, and thought at the very least Mrs. Wells would have removed Tyrone by force, but she didn't, endearing her to Baby Girl even more.

The next time she encountered Jill she was daydreaming and didn't notice her. As she descended the hill on her way home, Jill saw her first but pretended like she didn't and crouched down to tie her shoe. Jill pounced on her prey with a savage tackle, sending her tumbling, and the surprise in Baby Girl's eyes turned to fear when she realized her enemy was upon her. She quickly crawled to her feet but was pushed to the ground again with such force that she was convinced Jill had gotten stronger, so she decided to stay down. She rolled on her back and kicked her feet wildly whenever Jill tried to attack her. Some of her classmates were in the crowd now, and she noticed a boy that she beat in a spelling contest, winning a toy as a result. He seemed to enjoy seeing her scampering in the dirt, and smiled as he mockingly shook his head as if to say, poor girl. This enraged her and she wished Jill would get close enough so she could kick her hard, but Jill seemed content to dance around her victim, feigning an attack, then withdrawing just to see her miss. She laughed because it was just a game to her. Knowing her victim was not a threat pleased her. She knew all she had to do was wait for her to tire, then she would humiliate her, but she grew excited, impatient, and craved to punch her prey, causing her to become careless and wander too close. Suddenly Baby Girl stretched out and kicked Jill in the shin as hard as she could.

"Aaaaaah!" Jill yelled, then limped backwards.

She couldn't believe her good fortune and sprang to her feet, then gathered her books and backpack. Jill was so angry she still tried to get to her, even though she was hurt, she limped, then hopped to move faster, but it was no use because Baby Girl quickly retreated to the safety of her home.

A few days later she did see Jill, after school, and was glad that things were different this day because Jill did not see her. She figured she had a chance to escape and tried to mingle amongst her friends and use them as camouflage. As soon as she walked by Jill, she planned to run home, but her classmates were afraid and their group started to separate as they drew near, leaving her exposed, then her nervousness caused her to panic and she hastily burst from the crowd. Jill was startled but soon recognized what was happening and pursued her prey. Her shin was better now, and since they hadn't reached the mountaintop, running uphill slowed Baby Girl. Just as Jill was about to catch her, she started to run in a zigzag pattern, swiftly darting from left to right outside of Jill's reach, angering her predator, causing Jill to trip and stumble about while attempting to catch her. Instead of trying to reach out and grab her victim, the predator realized Baby Girl was close enough to trip, and skillfully did so with a leg sweep, sending her prey tumbling, causing holes in the ground as dirt and grass flew about. Jill quickly jumped on her so as not to repeat the scenario that happened during their last fight. She lay on her prey and wrapped her arm around her neck, placing her head in a choke hold, pulling back hard, but Baby Girl was able to grab Jill's forearm with both hands and resisted, positioning them under her chin to keep Jill from putting her forearm directly on her throat. This maneuver worked and Jill began wallowing on top of her victim and screaming,

"How you like it little pig! You wanna' choke somebody?! I got you now little pig! How's that feel, huh!"

She was humiliated as she heard the laughter from the crowd of kids and knew that her classmates were among them, but she was face down just above the dirt and couldn't see them.

"I didn't choke you. It wasn't me. It was Pam. You know it was Pam. You know it wasn't me…" she mumbled, still struggling to keep Jill's arm away from her throat.

"I don't care! She ain't here so you gonna' git' it!" Jill screamed, and forced her victims' face into the ground, laughing as her prey struggled. Baby Girl didn't cry. She was tough, emotionally, and grew angry as she kicked her legs and turned her head sideways out of the dirt. Suddenly she felt the weight come off her, and rolled onto her back to see her persecutor being pulled by an elderly man.

"Get off me old man!" Jill yelled, but the man was strong and he held her tight.

"I'm tired of you kids always fightin! You go ta' school ta' learn," he said. Baby Girl brushed the dirt and grass from her hair and face, and collected her things.

"Thank you, mister...." She said to her savior and ran away as he continued to hold her abuser.

She was tired now, emotionally and physically. In her weakened state, depression crept into her heart causing sadness and uncertainty. She needed help and even though her mother was suffering too, she needed her. She was almost home when she stopped running. She walked into the valley to enter Hilltop, which was part of the Dayton Metropolitan Public Houses. Tall buildings surrounded the two, story homes. The houses were identical, with beige aluminum siding covering the front, and red brick covering the sides and rear. The houses were not connected or fenced in. The backyards were open and you could see and walk the length of the block by passing through each backyard. There was no parking in the complex. Everyone had to park on the hill above, outside the complex, and walk in, using the sidewalks to guide them to their destinations, be it houses or buildings. There were no steps in front of her home and no doorbell.

When she entered her home, she moved quietly upon hearing Herby crying. He was sitting on the floor in front of their mother who sat on the couch, chewing crushed ice, watching T.V. They didn't hear her enter so she peaked into the doorway to investigate.

"Mama, mama, wus' wrong? Wus' wrong with you mama? Wus' duh' madda' mama? Wus' wrong? Mama, mama, mama wus' wrong? Mama, don't cha' hear me? Talk ta' me, say sumthin' mama, please mama, please talk ta' me, please mama, please say sumthin'...."

Herby wailed as tears cascaded down his cheeks and collected at his chin. He was rocking back and forth, sitting on the floor with his legs crossed, looking directly into his mother's eyes, but she ignored him and stared off in the distance, not watching the television rather gazing above it. Baby Girl couldn't watch any longer and decided to intervene. Her depression was suddenly gone when she realized her little brother was helpless and even though she was very young, she knew she was capable of caring for him. She closed the front door hard so he could hear it.

"Tee-Tee, Pam's outside playin' and mama won't help me. I'm hungry!"

Herby ran up to his sister and hugged her. He held her tight and she needed that. She needed to feel love. She needed to feel wanted. It soothed her pain and removed her sorrow, even if it was only temporary. She took Herby by the hand and led him to the kitchen which was in the back of the house. The homes in Hilltop were constructed where the lower level contained the living room and kitchen, while the second floor contained the bedrooms and bathroom.

"Sit here. I'm gonna' get Candace."

"Good, She's been fussin' all day. I tried ta' tell mama but she crazy."

"Don't say that!"

"But she is Tee-Tee!"

"I said don't say that. You don't know what happened."

Herby shrugged and sat in the chair. He didn't know what happened and he didn't care. All he knew was that he was hungry and his mother was ignoring him. That was the worst part for him, being ignored, he knew something was wrong. He knew if a person ignored you, they had to be mad at you, or they didn't see you, but for any other reason they had to be crazy. To look right through a person was strange to him, and being only three, it was frightening too. It was frightening because he felt alone and wasn't sure if his mother would save his life, but he knew his sister would. Herby loved and depended on her first, before anyone.

The next morning Baby Girl decided to talk to her mother about Jill. She got dressed and Pam got dressed too, to her surprise, because she never knew what her sister would do, but lately, when she stopped waking her, Pam was confused, then hurt, and felt that her guardian didn't care, or worse, that she had done something to offend her. After gathering her siblings, she took them downstairs to the kitchen and set the table with each child's cereal, then she returned upstairs to talk to her mother. She entered her mother's room to find her sitting in bed, fumbling with the sheets. She sat on the edge of the bed. Her mother ignored her.

"Mama, I got trouble at school. There's this big girl that's pickin' on me. Every time I see her, she wanna' fight, and she's too old ta' be fighting me. She in the sixth grade! Mama, you listening mama!"

Her mother began to slowly rock in bed now, continuing to fumble with the sheets, but she didn't look up. Suddenly Pam burst into the room for she had snuck behind her sister and was impatiently listening at the door. Pam was more animated than Baby Girl and wanted to tell her side of the story.

"Yeah ma! She been messin' wit' me too. Huh' name is Jill! She a big o' girl. She be fightin' us all the time! She be beatin' on Tee-Tee real bad. I jumps in when I'm round but she strong ma! She be beatin' both of us!"

Their mother seemed aggravated now and twisted the sheets tightly in her hands as she quickly raised her head, while angrily looking at her daughters.

"Well beat her ass," she replied sternly.

"But mama we can't!" the girls replied in unison.

"I told you, she big. I can't beat her. Can't you do something. You never do nothing anymore!" exclaimed Baby Girl.

"I said.... beat her ass. I didn't say fight her. If she mess wit' you, you pick up whatever you can find and hit her wit' it. Hit her hard now, and keep hittin' her. I bet she won't mess with you no more."

Baby Girl was shocked by her mother's advice but Pam seemed amused.

"I can't do that, I'll get in trouble!"

There was no reply for their mother was gone again. Her mind shut down and a blank stare returned. She always said that Baby Girl was born grown, and having conversations with people at the age of two, so this put her mind at ease when she left her in charge. Baby Girl got off the bed knowing her mother wouldn't help, then stomped out of the room with Pam trailing her.

"What we gonna' do Tee-Tee?"

"I don't know."

"You heard what mama said. Imma' bust her in the head with sumthin."

"No you ain't. You wanna' get in trouble."

"I don't care. I ain't scared. I'll bust her in the head."

"Come on now let's eat. I gotta' make sure Candace is clean before we leave."

"I wanna' go Tee-Tee. I can fight!" yelled Herby.

She smiled but didn't answer him. Herby and Pam started talking about all the different ways they would attack Jill if she messed with them. They were excited and happy as they schemed, so she sat at the table amongst her loved ones and quietly ate. She was pleased to have someone that would fight with her, even if they were only babies. The loneliness she felt when leaving her mother's room was gone. Her despair was soothed by her siblings' love.

It had been a while since she had seen Jill and Baby Girl was happy. She figured it was about two weeks since their last fight. During that time, she thrived at school, getting excellent marks on her test in Math and English. She was showing Pam one of her papers as they ascended the hill on their way home, it had a bright red "A+" on it. Pam suddenly froze, staring straight ahead with her eyes fixed in the distance. She knew without looking that it was Jill, and her predator saw them too. Jill smiled slyly, and rubbed her hands together as if to say, let's eat. She did not run towards them this time. She waited, patiently walking alongside them, but not too close as to startle her prey. Baby Girl pulled her sister along but suddenly Jill darted towards them as they approached the summit. Pam was afraid and wrestled free from her sister's grasp, then turned towards Jill and froze again, this time on purpose, like a statue, with her arms at her side and head towards the sky, she pretended she was invisible, since she was only five it made sense to her. She figured Jill was stupid and it would confuse her, and it did. Baby Girl couldn't believe it. She watched as her predator approached Pam, paused, then pushed her to the ground and ran past her. She couldn't believe Jill was that dumb, but she was too scared to try it. When Jill caught her, she betrayed her sister because she was afraid and tried to save herself.

"Pam's the one you want! I didn't do nothing! Look, she over there. You ran right past her. She the one you want!" Baby Girl yelled, as her abuser forced her to the ground and wrestled on top of her.

"Shut up!" screamed Jill. She looked back to see Pam running up to them. When Pam saw Jill looking, she froze again, causing Jill to frown and return to humiliating her victim. By this method of running, and stopping, and freezing, Pam was able to get into the crowd that surrounded the fight and quickly pounced on Jill from behind, but when she jumped her abuser stood up, causing Pam's chin to smash into the back of Jill's head, dropping Pam to the ground instantly. The blow was so hard that Jill held her head as she tripped backwards over Pam's lifeless body. She kicked Pam before she knew what happened, thinking Pam hit her with something, but when she realized Pam wasn't moving, she yelled to the crowd and pranced around her victims.

"Knock out! Knock out! Knock out! You got knocked the hell out!"

Jill chanted, and ran with the crowd down the hill leaving her victims to suffer. Some of Baby Girl's classmates lingered around not knowing what to do, and some even said that Pam was faking.

"Look right dare' she breathin."

"She suppose ta' be breathin' she ain't dead."

"Naw, she look like she sleep."

"Put ya' finga' unda' her nose."

"What for? You can see her chest movin."

"Oh, right."

"Well, put yo' finga' on her neck, like dey' do in duh' movies."

"Y'all git' from round' here!" She had enough of their questions and chased her classmates away, then knelt down and cradled Pam's head in her lap and waited. She didn't try to shake her sister or smack her. She was content feeling Pam's heartbeat until she awoke.

By October, Jill was still attacking the sisters. On this day Baby Girl was fortunate because some senior boys pulled Jill off her. Even her classmates stopped watching the beatings since now they pitied her, but were afraid to intervene and draw Jill's wrath. Pam rarely went to school after their abuser knocked her unconscious, although Baby Girl loved school too much to let fear keep her away, the bullying was taking its toll and weakening her spirit since she was trying to raise her siblings, attend school, and constantly fight her oppressor.

On this day, she was surprised to see her sister walk along side of her on the way home from school. She didn't know if Pam attended because she didn't leave the house with her. Usually if they didn't walk together, Pam wouldn't go at all.

"Tee-Tee, we ain't got no food."

"What are you talking about? Where did you come from? You went to school today?"

"Yeah, I did. I left after you. I was late but I went. You gotta' go shoppin' and get us some food."

"Okay, I'll go when we get home."

"Good, I'll help."

"I don't want you stealing nothing."

Pam didn't answer because that was a promise she couldn't make.

"Hey babies! Where y'all goin?!

The sisters were startled since they were too concerned with hunger to be wary, but it was too late, their enemy was upon them and Jill quickly grabbed Baby Girl by the hair and placed her in a head lock, then walked around with her prey trapped under her arm, humiliating her.

"Yeah, little baby! I got you now little baby! You can't do nuthin!"

Pam learned her lesson from their last encounter and began scanning the area, as her mother's words echoed in her mind. She saw a big stick in the brush and ran to retrieve it. A crowd had gathered to witness Jill taunt Baby Girl, so Pam snuck into the group of children, dragging her stick along the ground behind her as she stalked her abuser. No one noticed her weapon when she burst from the crowd. Since Jill had turned away, Pam began whipping her on her back. At first Jill was afraid, but realizing she wasn't hurt, she became angry and released her victim to exact revenge on Pam, attempting to chase her. Baby Girl tripped Jill with a foot sweep and sent her tumbling to the ground. Now Pam stopped her retreat and returned to beat Jill with the stick. The crowd of kids screamed with excitement and started to chant,

"Fight! Fight! Fight!"

Jill lay on her back, covering her face with her arms, trying to grab the stick, and finally she did, wrestling with Pam for its possession. Baby Girl couldn't let that happen so she kicked Jill like she did before, in the same knee as before, causing her enemy to release the stick and grimace in agony. Pam was mean and liked to cause pain, so she continued to hit her abuser even after her sister had run away, retreating only when the stick broke.

VII

THE STONING

It was the beginning of November and the two sisters were busy sorting the candy they received a few days earlier on Halloween. Since their mother was unconcerned about their health, they were giddy and high on sugar for three days. They were unsupervised. Aside from Baby Girl's guidance there were no rules at all. Their mother stayed home all day silently ignoring them. She didn't feed, cloth, or care for any of her four children, which was especially dangerous since the youngest child was only thirteen months. She didn't bathe herself, or comb her hair, or brush her teeth. She was sloppy, and unconcerned about her appearance because depression enslaved her.

With three fights in Baby Girl's classroom, it was a raucous school day. She was in the midst of the circus her classroom had become, but stayed focused on her school work. Since Melanie witnessed the beatings, she felt sorry now, because she knew her older sister wouldn't stop tormenting Baby Girl. Melanie wanted her to know that she was peaceful, but since she was only seven, she didn't know how to say it, so she started sharing her books and toys with her, silently pushing her things onto her classmate's desk since they sat across from each other, and she stopped saying Jill was going to get her. Baby Girl understood Melanie's gestures of friendship and was relieved, because the last thing she wanted to do was fight her too.

"Give me that Lewis!" yelled Mrs. Wells, while snatching a toy from his desk and handing it back to the student it belonged to.

"I told you about taking things from students. Now go sit in the corner!"

Lewis was a bully, and every day he would pick on various classmates, usually taking what he wanted from them. He was an eight, year old, light brown, heavy set, medium height boy, who didn't come to school to learn, and as a result, he was repeating the second grade. He only came to school to push and scare his classmates.

There was a commotion in the pencil sharpener line and one of the students got knocked to the floor and started crying. The culprit was Tyrone, who had his back to the pencil sharpener, guarding it from his classmates who were trying to use it. Mrs. Wells ran over to comfort the child and chastise Tyrone. The teacher's calm and caring demeanor was frazzled by the chaos in her classroom, but it was almost recess and she was looking forward to the quiet time.

During lunch the second graders ran, played, screamed, yelled, and rid themselves of rambunctious behavior in the school yard, so when they returned to class and were directed to sit and perform mathematics and reading, they complied. Some students slept at their desk while others sat quietly. Considering how disruptive they were before recess the teacher was relieved now because the children were calm. Mrs. Wells reminded Baby Girl of her mother when she was loving, before depression rendered her mind helpless.

Earlier that morning, before leaving for school she deviated from her normal morning routine. Since the garbage can in the kitchen was full, she threw the trash out, which she usually did later in the week for it was only Tuesday. She felt the chill of the brisk air rush over her as she closed the aluminum can and paused, transfixed on the mahogany brick that covered the sides and rear of her home. She was unaware of her actions as she just stood there, frozen, spellbound, her thoughts gradually drifting to fear and dread, which never happened before. She was usually excited to go to school because it was the best part of her day. In school she had her independence. After taking care of her siblings for so long, she welcomed situations where she was only responsible for herself. In class she could be as smart as she wanted, and was encouraged, and her knowledge was nurtured. She enjoyed this, being intelligent, it was her armor. She knew she could think her way out of any situation, and find the answer to any problem, but today her confidence was gone because she couldn't find a solution to make her predator stop abusing her. She wished she was hard like the brick that she stared at intensely, transfixed on the texture, rubbing her hands over it, then punching it softly with her fist as she mumbled to herself.

"I wish I was you, hard like you, strong like you..." she mumbled repeatedly, then began to rant, "If I was hard like you, I would be so strong that Jill could never hurt me. I'd hit her so hard. I'd knock her to the ground, I'd step all over her, I'd sit on her, I'd be so heavy, I'd crush her, and kick her, and punch her, and bite her."

Pam became curious since her sister was outside for a long time and braved the cold to witness her mumbling to herself, and softly punching the wall. Since Pam was a child, she wasn't alarmed and thought it was funny. She didn't know her sister was having a nervous breakdown because she never saw her vulnerable. After Baby Girl took their mother's roll as head of household, Pam never saw her distraught.

"Tee-Tee, come inside! We gotta' get ready!" Pam yelled, startling Baby Girl, waking her from her trance, as she returned to the house to help her infant sister finish eating. She wanted to make sure Candace had clean clothes and a fresh pamper before leaving.

As the school day drew to a close, the students collected their belongings in anticipation of the bell that signaled their departure. When the alarm sounded the students raced down the hallways, screaming and yelling as they ran to various exits. Some of the boys in the sixth grade took this opportunity to chase down the girls they liked and feel them up, touching the girls developing breast, smacking them on the butt as they ran, tackling them, sometimes humping on them as the girls squealed and struggled to get up. The popular girls were chased by several boys, as some of the less desirable girls looked on with envy, running slower, hoping to get caught, and when they were bypassed by a boy they liked, they would run to their girlfriend's aid, only to be felt up by the boy in order to make them leave, but this was what they really wanted so they stayed and wrestled with the boy. Some of the girls got felt up daily during this mad dash to the exits, and classmates called them nasty because the girls enjoyed being groped, as two or three boys would grab them at one time. The second graders were not being fondled since most boys weren't attracted to girls at this age. If a boy chased a girl in her class, it was to pull their hair, not smack them on the butt.

"Tee -Tee you ready? I got sumthin' for Jill if she messes with us today," Pam said, and collected rocks as they walked home, stuffing them into her book bag.

"I'm ready. Maybe she didn't come to school today."

"It don't matter. Sometimes she don't even go ta' school an

still waits at the top of the hill. She ain't got nuthin' betta' ta' do than pick on kids anyway. She mean."

"Well, we'll see if she's there. If she wants to fight, I'll kick her real good. I'm not playing today."

"That's right. You kick her and I'll bash her in the head."

"No. I told you about that. You gonna' get in trouble."

"It can't be any worse than gettin' beat up. Anyway, I'm tired of fightin' her. She too big ta' be pickin' on us. She in the six, grade. I don't know how you take it. She always hittin' on you."

"I know, I'm tired too. Maybe she does need to be hurt really bad, but I can't do that."

"I can!"

"It sure was something when you got that stick last time and was whooping her with it," Baby Girl said, and smiled as she recalled their last fight with Jill.

"I got her good, didn't I?!"

"You sure did. You would think that would make her stop but she just gets meaner."

"I know. We need ta' get some older kids ta' beat her up. I know some but they won't listen to me. You know any?"

"I wish mama was better. She would take care of Jill. She'd make sure Jill wouldn't hit us anymore."

"Mama can't do nuthin' she sick. She can't help nobody."

The sisters continued to walk in silence now, wishing their mother was healthy, wishing Jill would stop tormenting them. They trudged up the hill slowly, quietly contemplating their circumstances and were greeted by a familiar sight as they reached the summit. It was Jill. She had her back them as she talked to her friends. They attempted to continue home unnoticed but one of the girls Jill was talking to pointed them out. Jill flashed a menacing smile. The sisters walked together at first, but gradually separated as Jill approached because they wanted to see who she would attack. Their separation was more from fear than a strategic maneuver. Since they were bored and wanted to see some excitement, the school children were anxiously anticipating a fight and jostled amongst themselves for a better view, with wide eyes and joyful laughter. Now the predator attacked, chasing Pam, to Baby Girls surprise.

"You wanna hit me with a stick! Imma' git' you now little pig!" Jill yelled as she ran after her. Pam was slowed by the weight of her book bag because of the rocks she stored inside, and just as Jill was about to grab her she dropped it and zigzagged across the field with speed, circling back to her sister, whose fear had subsided as she gradually grew angry from the sight of her defender being pursued, since it was Pam who originally came to her aide when Jill assaulted her two months ago, and she wasn't about to let her only ally be harmed.

    Baby Girl ran behind Jill, and when she was close, she tackled her predator by the ankles and held on tight. Jill was surprised as she tumbled to the ground, and the children exuberantly screamed and yelled because it was unexpected since they had always seen her beaten. Pam didn't know what happened, and when she finally realized Jill wasn't chasing her, she was on the other side of the hill. She could hear the commotion and became curious because she didn't see her sister, so she cautiously returned to the summit and saw the crowd of children jumping around as they looked to the ground. Pam knew it was the girls fighting and ran back for a closer look. Jill was trying to break free of her victims' grasp as she lay on the ground, by punching and hitting her on the head. She couldn't hit her in the face because Baby Girl kept her head down, but eventually Jill was able to wrestle one leg free and kicked her prey hard on the shoulder.

    The children cried out, "Ohhhh!" But Baby Girl didn't release Jill's other leg. Again, as she lay on the grass with her victim holding onto one leg, Jill stomped down hard, this time hitting her on top of the head. The children cried out again, "Ooooh!" But no one came to her aide. They just watched the assault. Pam grew nervous now since she knew her sister was hurt, but she couldn't find her backpack and forgot where she dropped it. Again, Jill viciously stomped her in the head, and this time Baby Girl did peek, because the pain was severe and she wanted to see her surroundings. She caught a glimpse of her abuser, as they made eye contact Jill growled and raised her foot to stomp her again, and she quickly tucked her head down to brace herself for the blow.

    It was then that Pam saw it. It was partially covered with dirt and grass but she knew it was there, and ran over to retrieve it. It was a stone, and she picked it up with two hands because it was heavy, then ran back to the crowd, making her way through the children she lifted the stone high above her head to everyone's surprise. She stood behind Jill, who was too busy assaulting her sister to notice, and slammed her in the head with the stone, just above her right, ear, smashing Jill on the temple and immediately causing blood to trickle down her face as a knot appeared. Jill screamed in agony while holding her head, and stopped kicking her prey. Baby Girl was in shock and let go of her tormentor's leg as she watched her abuser rolling on the ground screaming and crying. Pam helped her sister stand, then took her by the hand and led her down the hill.

The crowd of children screamed their approval since it was thrilling to see such an event. Some of the younger children had never seen blood during a scuffle. They cheered and some of them walked alongside congratulating the sisters on their triumph, while revealing that they never liked Jill, and were happy she was hurt because she had tormented them too. Baby Girl was too upset to speak to them because they never helped her during the fight. She was angry and knew the children were pretending to be her friend.

As the sisters approached Hilltop Houses and walked into the valley, there was a commotion in the rear of the crowd and Pam instinctively started to run, pulling her sister along, not looking back because she was near their home. When the girls did reach their house, they stopped and turned to see their tormenter standing at the entrance of the public houses. Jill was pressing her hand against her head to stop the bleeding on the knot that swelled into a lump. She violently screamed at the sisters, threatening them as a small group of kids from a neighboring complex stood behind her.

Baby Girl was surprised, and scared, because Jill had never ventured down the hill to the valley. She heard Jill's taunts but didn't respond because she didn't want to provoke her tormentor. She was curious as she noticed Jill look past her, so she turned to see her siblings in the doorway. Pam had a hammer in her hand and Herby held a large kitchen knife. She turned back to Jill who continued to scream as she gradually backed away. She didn't want her siblings to get in trouble, so she quickly ushered them inside before they hurt someone.

"Didja' see that Tee-Tee!" Herby exclaimed. He was excited for it was the first time he saw his sisters' bully and was happy he could help them, deciding to take the knife because he knew it would frighten Jill.

The next day, after school, Baby Girl decided to eliminate the possibility of having to fight. She finally realized that she had the power to avoid this conflict, and did the only thing she could to protect them. After school she took Pam by the hand and proceeded to walk in the opposite direction, around the hill that separated them from home. She knew it was a much longer route but it was the only way she could be sure that a fight wouldn't occur since no children walked this way. Pam exhaled heavily in anticipation of the long journey but didn't protest, because she was tired of fighting too, and afraid that Jill might have a weapon this time.

VIII

SCHOOL'S CLOSED

Pam was tired of going to school. She was tired of walking the long way home. She was tired of getting up early on these cold winter days. All she wanted to do was watch T.V. and play, but her sister was an obstacle. Her sister loved school and attended daily, waking her siblings every morning. Pam hated this because she wanted to sleep late so she decided to tell her sister a lie.

"School's closed," she said.

"What do you mean?" Baby Girl asked and stopped washing the dishes.

"School's closed today. There's no school."

"Why you say that?" Baby Girl looked confused. Herby and Candace played at the kitchen table while Pam waited to see her sister's reaction.

"I didn't hear anything about school being closed today."

"Not just for today, it's all week," Pam replied, when she realized her sister might believe her, she lied even more.

"You know how we were out for Christmas and winter recess, it's like that."

"But it's March. School never closes in March. I'm gonna' ask mama."

"What for? She don't know."

Pam tried to sound as if she didn't care. She was a good liar and knew it was better to stay calm and appear uninterested. Baby Girl knew Pam was right about their mother and decided not to ask her. She was relieved, to her surprise, and thought of this as an unexpected treat, after all her hard work she felt she deserved a break, and gradually relaxed as she sat with her family at the kitchen table.

"Let's join hands."

"What for?"

"Come on, it'll be fun."

"Tee-Tee, Candace's hands are sticky!" exclaimed Herby.

"Well wipe them off. You can help her too. I don't have to do everything."

"Ok," Herby replied as he took a paper towel and rubbed his baby sister's hands while she giggled from his touch. She was in a playful mood because she enjoyed when her siblings were together. The children held hands, then Baby Girl began to sway back and forth, pulling her sisters and brother from side to side, as they began to smile, she moved faster causing them to laugh. Candace squealed with excitement and Pam was happy because her lie was believed. Baby Girl excepted her sister's deceit and merrily enjoyed the morning.

Their mother shuffled into the kitchen and went to the freezer to get ice for her cup. She was quiet and ignored her children.

"Mama, school's closed today."

"School's closed all week."

"I mean, all week."

Their mother didn't reply. She stayed silent as she filled her cup with ice then dragged her feet, shuffling along to the living room, and sat on the sofa. She didn't turn on the T.V. She just sat there slowly rocking, chewing the ice and twirling a strand of her scraggly hair. Her children burst into the room and turned on the television, then Pam jumped on the sofa and grabbed the remote, commandeering the television. As Baby Girl looked from the kitchen, she noticed her mother seemed to be annoyed with her children being so close to her. She didn't know why her mother was agitated but she wanted everyone to be happy so she stepped down from the chair she used to reach the sink, and strolled into the living room and imitated her teacher.

"Now just because we home don't think we not gonna' have school. Imma' get the room ready and we gonna' do our studies," she said with her hands on her hips. Since she was short for her age, her mother's apron almost touched the floor, and her chubby caramel skin glistened from the dishwater.

"Oh mannnnn! I wanna' watch T.V!" exclaimed Pam.

"You can watch T.V. later," Baby Girl replied, and left to go upstairs to get their classroom ready. She used Herby and Candace's room since they didn't sleep there. The room consisted of one twin sized bed, a crib that was rarely used, a small table and chair set, a small artist easel and stool. Herby was excited to play school and struggled to carry his baby sister upstairs while Pam remained on the couch with her mother. She was happy at first but became upset because Ellen kept hitting her with her elbow. At first Pam was confused because she wasn't hit often, the blows occurred in thirty second intervals, but she was an intelligent child and realized that Ellen was hitting her on purpose, silently, harder with each blow as she looked away.

"Tee-Tee I'm coming!" Pam yelled, and quickly jumped off the sofa and ran upstairs. She thought her mother was crazy and was happy to get away from her. She knew her older sister, precious Baby Girl, was her savior, and although she didn't want to play school, she'd rather comply than be silently abused by her mother.

As the week progressed their mother gradually relaxed because her first born was home to take care of her children, keeping them away from her, she liked this. She didn't want to talk to them and wished they weren't there. She wished she was alone to wallow in her grief, but she wasn't. She was furious as she ignored the children her beloved had conceived with her before he abandoned them. His betrayal was too much for her mind to accept and it shut down as a result, only letting her accomplish the basic functions of eating and sleeping, while depression enslaved her heart, removing the love she had for her children.

Baby Girl grabbed Candace from her brother when they finally reached the top of the stairs, and carried the toddler on her hip. She loved her tiny little hands and soft skin. Candace held on tight with one hand, leaving the other free to dangle, and point at things, and sway to the rhythm of her sister's stride, bouncing with each step, resembling a cowboy on horseback as they strolled into the makeshift classroom with Herby following close behind.

"I got the coloring books you gave me. They're almost finished," he said.

"We not doing coloring right now. That's for fun. We gonna' go over the alphabet and do some counting and reading."

"But I can't read."

"You can't read yet, but I'll show you how."

Herby was excited as he got his books and sat at the small table that was used as their desk. Even though he was a toddler he still wanted to know everything his sister knew, and she was happy her brother embraced knowledge. Pam came into the room now, pouting, with her arms folded.

"Oooh, you late!" Herby yelled.

"Shut up! I didn't even wanna' come up here. Tee-Tee, mamma keep hittin' me! I can't even watch T.V. with her there. She crazy!"

"I told ya," Herby chimed in.

"Hush up with all that sass. There's no talking in class."

"You ain't no real teacher," Pam replied, as Herby giggled while holding his little hands over his mouth with his head down.

"I see you Herby. Now don't follow her. You wanna' be a good student when you go to school."

"I can't wait. Imma' know everything when I go ta' school. When will that be?"

"In about two years."

Herby sat up straight in his chair and opened his notebook and gazed at the blank pages as he thought about the two, years he had to wait to attend school. He had no concept of time but two years seemed like a lifetime away. Baby Girl used their drawing easel as the blackboard and enjoyed writing on the large paper canvass. It made her feel important as she stood before her siblings writing the letters of the alphabet.

"Ok, write the letters in your notebooks," she said, as Pam and Herby sat at the table while Candace sat on the floor, ruggedly turning the pages in her coloring book, trying to imitate her siblings. Since she was thirteen months old, she could only walk a few steps before falling, but her limited mobility made it easier for Baby Girl to monitor her movements. She had to be vigilant since Candace could crawl fast, and would occasionally try to sneak away when she wasn't looking. It was a game to her, and she squealed with excitement every time her sister caught her just as she crawled under the bed, then brought her back to the center of the room.

Herby grew frustrated as he struggled to write the letters, and frowned as he awkwardly fumbled with his pencil. When she was finished writing the letters of the alphabet on the easel, she went over to help her brother because she could see he was upset.

"It's not hard," she said and knelt down beside him. The two chairs and matching table were small because they were made for children ages two to five, so when she knelt next to her brother, she was just the right height to look over his shoulder and help him.

"See, your notebook has three lines for each row. There are two solid lines on the outside, and one dotted line in the middle," she said, as she placed her book on the table next to him.

"I'll show you how to do it," she replied, and wrote the first few letters on the line below his. She used the three lines as she wrote two versions of each letter, one capital A, and one small a, and so on. The capital letters touched the third line and the small letters only touched the second dotted line, and were a different shape. Now Herby knew how to use the three lines and wrote the letters again, this time correctly.

"There you go. See, you can do it. When you're finished all the letters, I'll show you how to count."

"I know how to count Tee-Tee!" Herby exclaimed, "One, two, three, five, seven, eleven, ten, six… see I'm learning."

"Yes, yes you are," she couldn't help but laugh as Pam angrily looked on.

"That ain't right! You ain't countin' right dummy!" Pam yelled.

"What I tell you bout' all that sass? Now I see why you're not doing well in class."

"But he's not countin' right."

"Don't worry about what he's doing. You worry about your own work. If he's not counting right then you help him. You know how to count, don't you?"

"Yeah."

"Well, help him. Don't just wait for me ta' do it."

"Yeah, don't just wait for her ta' do it," Herby said, mimicking his older sister as she held his hand, and guided it to show him how to write correctly, causing him to giggled from her touch while making faces at Pam.

"Stop playing around. You have to be serious if you want to do good in school," Baby Girl replied, and continued to guide his hand.

"Why doesn't Pam do good in school?"

"I don't know. I think she talks back to the teacher and gets in trouble."

"You don't like school Pam?" Herby asked. He was genuinely concerned because he thought school would be fun, especially since all his friends would be there.

"It's okay, but my teacher don't like me. She mean."

Herby didn't understand this because he thought all teachers had to be friendly.

"Even though she's mean I still do my work. See, I can

write," Pam said, showing Baby Girl her notebook with the letters of the alphabet neatly written. She smiled and replied,

"I knew you were smart. You just misbehave, that's your problem."

Finally, it was Sunday evening and the children talked as she cleared the kitchen table.

"I had fun during the week but now I'm ready to go back to school."

"You can't. School's still closed."

"But you said it was closed for a week."

"I know, that was for the kids, but now it's closed cause nobody's there. You know, like when our favorite store closed, the one next to the park, like dat."

"But school can't close like that. What are all the kids and teachers gonna' do?"

"I dunno."

"You don't know what you're talking about. I'm gonna' ask mama."

"She won't know."

"Well, I'm gonna' ask her anyway."

She was confused and a little worried as she walked up the stairs to her mother's bedroom. What if school was really closed? What would she do? She couldn't imagine life without school, it was her sanctuary, even though she had trouble with a bully in the beginning of the year, she still needed to get away from home because this was the only time, she could be independent. She yearned for the nurturing, guidance, and encouragement from her teacher.

Her mother's room was dark and the curtains were closed blocking out the early evening light. The door was partially closed and Baby Girl knocked a few times before pushing it open.

"Mama, you awake?" She asked loudly, but there was no answer. She peered into the darkness. When her eyes adjusted, she could see her mother lying in bed with the covers pulled over her head. She was determined to get an answer so she entered the room and turned on the light. Her mother moaned with disapproval. As she approached the bed, the odor of excrement, armpits, and feet, assaulted her nostrils, and kept her from moving any closer.

"Mama, Pam said school's closed, but we already been out a week and she said it's still closed. That don't sound right. Mama, you hear me?"

"I hear ya'. I hears ya' jus' fine," her mother mumbled.

"I don't think Pam knows what she's talking about. I'm going to school in the morning and find out for myself."

"If she say school's closed then it's closed. It's too cold ta' be walkin' ta' school if it's closed. You jus' stay here an teach dem' like you been doin', school will be open soon, you'll see," her mother lied, being unconcerned with her daughter's desires. She was selfish and wanted to be free of her children, knowing everything would be cared for while Baby Girl was there. She didn't care about her daughter's happiness, taking advantage of her first born seven, year old, because she knew it was irresponsible to place such a burden on a child.

"Tina you gonna' see that everythin' in life ain't always good. But you gotta' accept some things… and move on. Now I'm restin' so turn that light off and leave me be…"

Baby Girl lowered her head and turned off the light as she left the room. She was relieved to be away from her smelly mother, who she was ashamed of, and happy to go downstairs and return to her siblings, whom she loved. She knew they depended on her so she did her best to take care of them. She made sure they were feed, bathed and taught. She didn't know her actions were saving the family. All she knew was that her mother was in trouble, she was sick, and someone needed to do all the things she was unable to. It made her feel important to be able to help because she knew a child her age was never allowed to roam free, unsupervised, unrestricted, unabated, without parental guidance, but since her father had abandoned them, she was thrust into this role and to her families benefit she flourished at it. Her mother wasn't on drugs or an alcoholic, it was mental illness that caused her to breakdown.

"What y'all doin?" she asked when she returned to the kitchen, seeing Pam and Herby running around the table as Candace clapped joyfully.

"Pam took my spoon Tee-Tee. She won't give it back."

"See that's what I'm talking about. You always startin' trouble. I bet you do the same thing in school."

"Oh shut up! You don't know. What did mama say? Did you ask her? What did she say?"

"I asked her. She said school is closed."

Pam tried to hide her surprise since it was rare that

something surprised her. She didn't expect her mother to agree with her and was prepared to return to school. She didn't know why her mother lied, but she figured in her sick state, her mother really didn't know if school was closed. Regardless of the reason Pam was happy, and relaxed, and gave her brother his spoon, then ran into the living room to watch television since they wouldn't have to get up early the next morning.

There was no telephone in the house, no bell on the front door, and during the winter months the children stayed inside because the weather in Dayton, Ohio was very cold. The Hendrix family was shut away from the outside world, if not for the occasional trip to the grocer or laundry they rarely ventured out, so Baby Girl didn't communicate with her classmates, if she had, she would have discovered the truth. Her schoolmates would have told her that school was open, or at least they would have asked her why she wasn't going to school, and that's what happened on this fateful day. She had been out of school for almost a month when her family depleted their food. She had to go to the store for supplies and saw one of her classmates as she walked home.

"Hey Tina, where you been?" the boy asked.

"I been home since school's closed. What you been doing?"

"I been goin' ta' school. Who told ya' school was closed?"

"My sister."

The boy laughed immediately. "You know yo' sista' be lying. Why she tell you dat? School's not closed. You betta' go. You gonna' git' in trouble. Ain't nobody call yo' house from duh' school? They be callin' if you stay out too long."

"I don't know. We don't have a phone, but I'm going tomorrow."

"You betta' and yo' sista' betta' go too."

Now she was worried, and confused. She felt silly for believing Pam but she didn't understand why her mother would lie, after all, she did ask her and she said school was closed. She realized, even though they didn't discuss it together, Pam and her mother had lied to keep her home so she could do all the housework, the cleaning, and the shopping. She was angry when she returned, and silently prepared her clothes for school the next day. When the sun rose, she woke her siblings. Pam was surprised to see her clothes arranged on the bed but didn't ask any questions since she knew her lie was uncovered. Baby Girl silently prepared breakfast, as they ate Herby realized they were leaving.

"Y'all goin' ta' school today?" he asked. His sisters ignored him and he became upset because he hated to be ignored.

"Tee-Tee! Y'all goin' ta' school today? I wanna' go!"

"You know you can't go. You too young. Just take care of Candace while were gone," Baby Girl replied, then gathered her things and departed in silence. Pam rushed to keep up with her as they walked to school along with the other children from the neighborhood.

When she entered her classroom all the children stopped what they were doing and came to her. They surrounded her desk and expressed their concern about her absence. That's when she realized the severity of the situation. Her teacher, Mrs. Wells, came to her and hugged her gently, and stroked her back, and asked if everything was alright. Luckily, she was a good student and usually completed her assignments before they were due, so she was able to continue the second grade unhindered by her long absence.

"We tried to contact your mother but we were unable to. The principle sent a letter of inquiry to your home but there was no response. We thought you might have moved. Is everything ok?" Mrs. Wells asked.

"Yes mam. My mama was sick so I had to take care of her."

Mrs. Wells was shocked and didn't try to hide her expression. She couldn't understand how a seven, year old could be left with such a tremendous responsibility. She figured there was no father in the home, or any other adult because how else could such a thing happen. She feared her precious student was being abused, not physically, but mentally. That's the only conclusion she could reach under the circumstances. If Mrs. Wells knew the severity of Baby Girl's situation, she would have alerted child services, but since she did not, her motherly instincts took over, and she decided to love her student even more.

IX

BABY GIRL'S BIRTHDAY PARTY

It was July 20, 1977 and Baby Girl was celebrating her 8th birthday. Every year she was given a party at her aunt's house but this year the party was at her home. Aunt Mae, who lived in a two, bedroom house with her husband and two children, banned Baby Girl's family from visiting because they had a big fight at her annual 4th of July barbecue. Aunt Mae mistakenly thought they started the fight. She was so upset that she made Ellen cry. Since Mae was the older sister, being yelled at reminded Ellen of when they were little and Mae would chastise her. She began crying when Mae wouldn't stop accusing her children. Mae was calling them names and ordering them to leave. She kept yelling, "Take your bad ass kids and get outta' here!" Even though Ellen protested their innocence, Mae refused to listen because there were numerous times in the past when they were the culprits.

The fight began when Baby Girl's cousin, Curtis, threw a pop bottle and hit her in the ankle by mistake. He was aiming for his niece, Joann. The glass bottle hurt her and caused her to cry. Joann was teasing Curtis and everyone knew not to tease him because he was crazy. He was twenty, two, and moved to Ohio from Alabama after visiting for many years. It was common knowledge that he was unable to control his anger. Ordinarily the tall, slim, café complexioned man was quiet and unassuming, but when he was upset his anger turned to rage and hijacked his mouth and limbs, causing him to say and do violent things. The family would say he's certifiably insane but doesn't have the papers. Curtis had certain rules of conduct and if anyone violated those rules, family or not, he would scream at them, and if the conduct continued, he would hit them. Baby Girl knew how to deal with him because she was accustomed to crazy since her sister Pam was nuts, and a kleptomaniac. She only spoke to Curtis if she was greeting him, other than that she would only smile and wait for him to address her. Curtis liked her and always came to her aid if she was being harassed.

She knew her cousin, Joann, was mean, ornery, and

unafraid of Curtis, well, she was afraid but unconcerned about his feelings. Whenever she made him angry, she would run knowing he would attack her. She never smiled and always talked bad about people. She was eighteen, short, fat, and unattractive, with hair so short it only made a pigtail. She had an onyx complexion and the family said she was darker than coal, they called it blue black, they said, "You can't get no blacker'n dat'. When she closes her eyes'n duh' dark you can't see er!" Baby Girl didn't know the reason for Joann's terrible attitude but it was said that she had a rough childhood. Whatever the reason she was evil, and liked to make others miserable. Joann, like Curtis, moved to Ohio from Alabama with her mother, after visiting for many years. In fact, all the family on Ellen's side were migrants from Alabama, who moved north for a better life.

Every year Aunt Mae invited the relatives from the south to visit, even though she didn't have enough room. They were mostly from Greenville, and Mobile, Alabama. Her grandmother had eight children, which was normal for that period in time, the 1920's. The families were sharecroppers and had many children to help them work the farm, forsaking school, preventing their children from attending class past the age of thirteen so they could work fulltime in the fields, not understanding the need for more education, not understanding that there was another way to live, not realizing there was a life outside of their own. It was unfortunate because the landowners never paid them enough to live, and made a practice of extending credit to the sharecroppers, thus keeping them in debt. Only the brave ones ventured north because it was a dangerous trip magnified by the uncertainty of what lay ahead. They were pioneers who established a sanctuary in Ohio. They left Alabama with only the clothes they wore, and whatever parcels of food and water they could carry. They walked, hitch hiked, and stowed away on freight trains during their journey north, traveling to an unknown land with the belief that there was work, and a life free from debt and servitude.

Pam and Herby didn't care that their sister was hit with the bottle by accident. They saw her crying and retaliated by throwing rocks at Curtis and Joann, of course Aunt Mae came outside just in time to see them, and blamed them for starting the fight, kicking them out as a result. It was sad because Baby Girl didn't want to leave.

As a result of the fight Ellen and Mae weren't speaking, and Mae didn't attend the birthday party. Her children attended, driven there by her husband, but he dropped them off and didn't stay. Naturally Curtis and Joann weren't welcome. Baby Girl knew her party at home wouldn't be as good as the ones given at Aunt Mae's house because her aunt gave festive gatherings. She would always have a volleyball net set up in the backyard, where a cement patio was built to accommodate her guest, and a barbecue pit was constructed to accommodate large slabs of meat. There was a large Oak tree that sat in the back of the yard and the kids would carve their names in it. She enjoyed playing at Mae's house and wished they weren't banned.

Six cousins ranging in age from seven to seventeen came up every summer, when school was out, and stayed until September. To be exact, the six children were accompanied by three adults, making the total number of guests even larger. They would all cram into a minivan and make the sixteen, hour commute, stopping along the way to rest, bathroom breaks, and various things. It was easy because they shared the driving. Sometimes Mae's husband, Morris Sr., would drive down to get them, but it was only when he felt up to it, since it was an arduous trip and he traveled alone. The six children that visited most often, since sometimes the occupants changed, were Judy, Ann, Anita Baby, Todd, Tanky and Mobey. Out of this group Mobey visited the most, starting at age seven and ending when he was eighteen. He was two years younger than Baby Girl and was killed at the age of twenty, one, as a result of street violence. It was unbelievable that this was an annual visit since Mae really didn't have room for them. All her guest would cram into her home where pullout beds were used in the living room, and bed rooms.

Baby Girl's six cousins attended her birthday party, along with her siblings, and three friends she invited from the neighborhood. She wore her favorite outfit, a pink Capri pant suit with a shirt that tied at the ends, accompanied by white sandals. She especially liked the shirt because it tied at her waist, which was different from regular shirts. She was enjoying her day, running and playing with the children. Since she was mature for her age she played with the older kids. Her siblings didn't care because they were happy to run, jump, yell, and scream to their hearts content. They were unhindered by adults, or parental guidance, since their mother was still suffering from depression and mostly stayed inside on this warm and sunny day.

    Her friends arrived amongst this chaos of fun and wanted to join in the festivities only to be confronted by her cousins. It was customary for guest to attend the party in dress clothes but her friends were unaware of this. They were happy and jovial when they arrived only to be met with insults. Anita Baby answered the door and immediately frowned when she gazed upon their common attire. Two girls and a boy stood there waiting to enter. One of the girls and her brother lived next door while the other girl lived down the street. They played with Baby Girl often but it was their first time meeting her cousins, who were older and intimidating. She didn't know they had arrived because she was busy playing in the backyard, but Pam ran to her side and informed her that they had come. By the time she could get to the front of the house the damage was done. The boy, who was younger, was already crying since he was sensitive and not accustomed to insults, but his sister was angry as they walked away with Baby Girl pursuing them. She wanted to know why they were leaving and was shocked when they told her what happened. She walked them back to the house and confronted Anita, who remained adamant.

    "They gotta' change dey' clothes if dey' wanna come in. Look at him. His clothes all dirty. He can't come in here like dat!"

    "No, they're my friends. You can't tell them not to come. I invited them. You can't tell them not to come. They're my friends!"

    Baby Girl, who was happy just a moment ago, now was in disbelief. She was ashamed that her cousins were treating her guests like this, after all, it wasn't their party since they were guest themselves. She couldn't control her emotions. She couldn't stop yelling, and her once mature demeanor was transformed to her current age, as she helplessly realized she couldn't prevent her tantrum. Now Herby and Pam observed the spectacle because it wasn't often, they saw her lose control. They stopped running around and watched since they knew this would be far more enjoyable. Their sister advanced from shouting and screaming to pushing and punching. Anita continued to stand in the doorway knowing she couldn't be moved by a little girl, since she was bigger and older, thirteen, she thwarted Baby Girl's punches with her hip because her lower body was thick, and absorbed the blows.

"Get outta' my house! If my friends can't come then you can't come either!" Baby Girl screamed, unaware that her friends had gone.

"Calm down. It's your birthday. Whatchu' cryin' for?"

"Nooo, you can't tell my friends not to come!"

Tears flowed and rested on the front of her blouse.

"look, dey' gone anyway. It's all for the best cause' dey' wasn't dressed right."

"You don't tell my friends how to dress. It's my party!"

Another cousin came to the door after she heard the commotion.

"What's all this noise about. What's wrong with Tee Tee. Why she cryin?" Judy asked.

"I told her friends dey' can't come to the party cause dey' ain't dressed right," Anita revealed.

"I know. Didja' see that boy? He was all dirty like he been rollin' in the grass."

That was it. She couldn't believe her cousins were in agreement. What upset her most was that they made her friends feel ashamed. She felt responsible because she wasn't aware her cousins were going to be inconsiderate and mean. She couldn't listen to them anymore as their words saddened and infuriated her, causing her to kick Anita in the leg and run.

Pam was excited now because the scene had escalated to complete chaos. Her animated demeanor enticed Herby, compelling him to run behind his sisters. Pam was delighted when she saw Anita limping after them, cursing as she hobbled about. Pam loved to be chased, especially when she knew she wouldn't be caught, being that Anita was injured and couldn't run fast.

"Come here you little devils!" Anita yelled.

Judy laughed as she watched the chase from the doorway. She never saw her act like this since Baby Girl always conducted herself in a responsible manner. The adults always said she acted like a little lady, being so smart and mature.

"Imma' whoop yo' butt when I catch you little demons!" Anita screamed, and hobbled after the children who ran to the back of the house. Their home was one of many two floor townhouses that formed a row and were surrounded by taller buildings that completed Hilltop.

"You ain't whopping nobody!" Pam yelled, and stopped

running long enough to pick up a rock and throw it at her, narrowly missing Anita's head.

"Girl, if that rock woulda' hit me…that's it! Your mine now! You think I'm playin! Your butt is mine now!"

"Ahh' hahh! That's what you get for messin' with my sista!"

"Ahh' hahh!" Herby chimed in. He couldn't help himself. The act of teasing someone delighted him since he wasn't the recipient of the taunts. He was elated and giggled as he ran. He wobbled, not because he was short and chubby, he stumbled about, not because he was five, but because he was drunk with happiness, holding his stomach because it ached from laughing so hard, until finally elation overcame his bodily functions and he pissed his pants as he collapsed to the ground. It wasn't a lot of pee, just enough to leave a stain on his light blue denim shorts, revealing his accident to Anita as she limped pass.

"Ewwww, you nasty!" she squealed. She wanted to kick him but it was too funny, so she just laughed as she watched him rolling in the grass trying to get to his feet, hindered by his loose, fitting shorts that were one size too big, and falling off his butt. His antics caused everyone's anger to subside. The sisters stopped running when they realized they were no longer being chased. They turned to see Anita standing over Herby as he squirmed to his feet while pulling up his shorts, revealing his pee stain.

"Oh, Herby peed himself!" Pam shouted as she pointed. Baby Girl was transformed from angry to amused at the sight of her brother.

"Ew, Herby's got the cooties!"

"No, I don't"

"Yes, you do!"

"No, I don't"

Every child knew that having the cooties was the worst thing, more than getting sick, or being punished, or even getting a whooping, because this ailment caused all the children to run away from you in fear of catching it. To avoid your touch was the goal thus alienating you.

"You got the Cooties!" Anita chimed in, joining the children, forgetting about the incident that brought them to this point. Herby was unaware that he had saved the day. He was just glad to be the center of attention, and touched his pee stain, and chased after the horrified girls with his outstretched hand.

"Mama... Herby being nasty!" they screamed and ran from the grassy knoll towards the house, but since Anita was hurt, she was the one to get caught. Even though Herby couldn't run fast he zeroed in on her like a wolf towards wounded prey.

"Stop! Herby Stop! I'm not playin' the game. You go and play with your sisters!"

"Yes you are! Den' why you say I got da' cooties!"

"No... seriously, I'm not playing. I'm not in the game." Anita tried to sound rational, and assertive, but to no avail.

"Yes you are! Den' why you runnin! Why you runnin' den!"

"No boy! Go and play with your sisters! See they're over there!"

"I see um', I see um'...............I see you too!" Herby smiled as he closed in on her, shortening the distance between them, gradually tracking her.

"No boy! I ain't playing! Don't you touch me! Get away from me! No! Get away! Nooooooooooo!"

Yup, he touched her, and she was mortified. She couldn't believe she was touched by the pissy hand of a toddler. It was too much for her to accept, and her reflexes caused her to push him away and kick him. Herby didn't care. He was a tough child, hardened since birth from fighting with Pam.

Suddenly Ellen appeared at the back door and called out to them, "Come on in y'all. We gonna' sing happy birthday and cut the cake!" The rest of the cousins were already inside waiting for them. Baby Girl and Pam entered first, followed by Anita. It seemed to take forever for Herby to enter. As soon as he walked in Anita screamed.

"No... he can't be here! He gotta' clean up first! Look at his pants!"

"Yo' man you too big to be pissin' your pants!" exclaimed one of the boys.

Herby just giggled and raised his hand slowly.

"Watch out! That's his pee hand! He touched his pee stain and chased us!" Anita shrieked.

The male cousins looked at Herby with disgust because they were teenagers and didn't play with babies. Upon seeing their expression Herby quickly put his hand down, but it was too late to stop his mother from slapping him in the head. He ceased laughing but didn't cry since he was more surprised than hurt.

"Imma' take him and get him cleaned up," Ellen replied. It was one of the few times she cared for one of her children. She did it in part because she didn't want her guest to know the severity of her depression. She even bathed and combed her hair for the party, and baked an enormous vanilla cake with creamy white frosting. While she was baking the cake, her children were in a festive mood because it had been a while since the oven produced such a delicious aroma that filled the house, and enticed them with thoughts of tasting the sugary treat. Soon Baby Girl forgot about her sadness as a result of her friends being dismissed.
Unfortunately, her amnesia was temporary as she was distracted by happiness. Any relief from dealing with her family was acceptable. She had no idea, on her eighth birthday, that she would have to leave Ohio when she became an adult, in order to save herself and her children. She was unaware that Pam would try to kill her. Presently she was happy and content since her party ended up being fun, in spite of her friends being banned.

X

THEY KILLED MY DOG

It was an innocent puppy. It didn't deserve to die like that, suffocated, smothered to death in an Easy Bake oven, trapped in this tomb by two children. The only crime was barking all night, every night, since the owner placed it in the backyard because it kept whimpering in the house, and caused her baby to cry. The children didn't mean to kill the puppy, they just wanted to muffle the noise and figured if they shut the oven tight, then they wouldn't hear the puppy barking. They were right, and forgot about the puppy as they played, and were proud for solving the problem that was keeping their neighbors awake at night, and left the scene only to have the owner discover their horrific crime.

The owner of the puppy was a young woman named Teresa. She was twenty, two, and moved six houses away from Baby Girl, four months ago. She lived with her boyfriend and her newborn son. Teresa was uncouth, rude, foul-mouthed, and uncivilized. She was slim, beige complexioned, with unattractive plain features, and short, auburn hair crowned her tall frame. She often wore dingy sweat pants and a head scarf. Her finger nails were grimy and the tips of some were discolored from smoking blunts all the way to the end, which are cigars filled with marijuana instead of tobacco. The sticky, brown, blunt residue stained her teeth, adding to her unattractiveness. Her only asset was her shapely firm buttocks, and she knew this, and highlighted it by shaking her hips, and switching excessively when she walked. She only wore sweat pants or jeans that were too tight. She'd squeeze into the jeans, barely able to zip them, pulling them tight into her butt crack, exposing the gap between her legs, since this was uncomfortable and caused her to get a yeast infection, she mostly wore sweat pants, but even this was scandalous because sometimes she wore them with no underwear, causing her hips to bounce freely. She never closed her legs when she sat. She'd lean back in her chair with her legs wide open while holding her baby when she was on her porch, or when she drank and smoked with her boyfriend after the baby was asleep.

When Teresa first moved there, she was bossy because she had a man while most of the other women were single mothers. She felt superior, and went from house to house telling the occupants to be quiet since she had a little baby and the noise would wake him.

"Y'all gotta' cut out all dat' noise!" she yelled, and banged on Baby Girl's screen door, and peered inside because the wooden door was open. Ellen just sat on the couch out of view, chewing ice from a cup, in a trance like state, ignoring her shouts. It was a bad day because her depression was severe and rendered her frozen. On days like this Baby Girl took control of the house, since she was dependable, and familiar with the responsibility.

Pam and Herby were running outside in front of Teresa's house, but they were on the sidewalk, not on her porch or in her walkway. They were playing with Herby's best friend Antwaan. The boys were five, rambunctious, and loved to run down the sidewalk racing each other. The fun started at Baby Girl's house. They lived in the corner house and had their own porch, all the other houses in the block shared a porch, only the corner houses had their own. The children gathered on the porch initially, but soon became too wild and felt hindered so they abandoned the porch for the sidewalk. Only Baby Girl would stay on the porch, playing with her toys quietly or reading a book, naturally she was on the porch when Teresa approached. The children were playing when the boys started arguing about who won the race. Pam was unconcerned because she was never in the lead during the races, she always trailed behind. The disagreement turned physical as the boys started shouting and tussling. The disturbance was so loud it caused Teresa to yell from her window.

"Y'all can't be playin' down here. Go up the street! Get from round' here!"

"I live right there, lady!" Antwaan replied, and pointed to the house next door. He didn't like her. No one on Wexford Place did.

"Don't chu' gimme' no backtalk boy! You betta' respect yo' elders!"

"You ain't my elder, booger lips!" Antwon shouted. The kids bestowed this nickname on Teresa because the marijuana residue gave her lips a mucky hue. Pam and Herby were shocked because no one ever called her that to her face.

"What chu' call me boy! I'll whoop yo' butt!"

Antwaan didn't care since he was already upset and flustered from fighting. He wasn't scared because when she came outside, she was holding her baby and he figured there wasn't much she could do to him while holding a baby.

"Imma' tell yo' mama, that's what Imma' do!" she shouted, and stormed pass the children, walking straight to Baby Girls' house.

"Is yo' mama home!" she shouted as she approached, but Baby Girl didn't answer. She just looked up and frowned.

"Who you frownin' at lil' heffer! All y'all bad ass kids is crazy! Well, I don't play dat! Y'all ain't gonna' be makin' noise like dat'. Wakin' my baby! Where yo' mama at!"

She screamed as she banged on the door but no one answered, and she eventually stormed off when Pam and Herby returned. It was hard for them to stop playing in front of Teresa's house, because the home was unoccupied before she moved there, and the porch was a favorite hangout for the kids.

This was the first day, it was a Wednesday and the sun was setting on this April, spring eve, when the tenants of Wexford Place met their new neighbor. She complained about other people making too much noise but everyday around this time at dusk, she smoked weed and drank alcohol on her porch until the early morn, playing her music and chatting with her friends who were mostly men, and acquaintances of her boyfriend. The ladies who attended always came with the men because Teresa had no female friends. Three days after moving in, on Saturday night, Teresa had a party. That's when the neighbors realized what kind of resident they really had.

She was young, unemployed, and living off Section 8, which was a welfare grant given to poor unwed mothers to help them in their time of need. Once a girl eighteen or older became pregnant, if they were destitute, they could apply for welfare from the state, and if approved Section 8 was granted. Social Services would find the mother an apartment and pay her rent for as long as she was on the program. The grant was meant to give the mother a chance to go to school, learn a trade, get a job, and leave the program. It was meant to be the financial support necessary for the mother to succeed, it was meant to fight the epidemic of teen pregnancy, but the women on Section 8 used the grant as a means to an end. They saw it as a way of life, not as a temporary solution. When girls came of age they already knew if they didn't want to work, or go to school, they could always get pregnant, get on welfare, and get Section 8. This strategy was senseless, abusive, and gave birth to a generation of babies that were financial pawns, created solely by lazy, ignorant, irresponsible people, for selfish reasons. The mothers receiving assistance would try to explain their actions by saying to their friends who were struggling, "Girl, why you working so hard and still living at home? You need ta' have a baby and get that Section 8."

    The recommendation to live on section 8 was given to many of the girls in Dayton Metropolitan Public Houses, by their friends, and some parents too, which was tragic because it became a cycle of welfare dependency that lasted for generations. The mothers used their knowledge of the welfare system to manipulate and abuse it. Instead of having one child and getting off the system, they would have a second child so they could stay on, never desiring to be independent or self, supportive. They would let their boyfriends move in with them illegally, because the men weren't on the lease. They would except money and gifts from the men and were content living this way. The state would ask for the father's identity. If the mother knew and revealed it, the state would go after him for child support, therefore, many mothers said they didn't know who the father was because the men were poor, and would leave them if they had to pay. Instead, the men became lazy too, knowing they could live with the mother rent free, in fact, many young men in the public houses preferred to be with ladies on Section 8 since they knew they had their own place. It was a scheme that was never intended to exist, and it corrupted all the participants, even the innocent children.

    The neighbors had no idea that Teresa would have a party every weekend with the same rowdy crowd, so by the third week they were unwilling to except her demands of quiet, when she herself was noisy mostly every night. On this weekend some of the men at the party started fighting. The commotion woke Baby Girl, so she looked out the front window from the second floor of her home and peered down the block to see the action. The men were in the street now and she could see Teresa pulling her boyfriend by the arm, leading him away from the fight. Suddenly sirens flared and red, white, and blue lights illuminated the room, bouncing off the walls as the police car approached. Two of the men that were fighting ran up the street towards Baby Girl's house, as everyone else scattered like roaches. Soon two more police cars arrived and stayed on the scene until the partygoers departed.

A month after moving in, Teresa's boyfriend, a muscular dark, skinned man of twenty, six, gave her a puppy as a present because he knew she always wanted a dog, therefore he promised to give her one when they got their own place. It was a female, black, pit bull with a white belly. Teresa named her Oreo, and cradled it just like she cradled her baby since the puppy was a newborn and couldn't walk yet. Teresa watched the pup grow as the weeks progressed, and now the dog whimpered every night before it fell asleep. The cries always woke her baby and she hated this because it delayed her time to hang out. Instead of consoling the puppy, and calming it, she showed her indifference by sitting it outside in the backyard, in the dark of night, rendering the already frightened puppy terrified. Now it no longer whimpered but barked freely, making a high pitched "arf" sound, for hours, until it fell asleep from exhaustion, every night.

It was on the second weekend of the puppy fiasco when the boys made their move. Herby and Antwaan already discussed their plan earlier as they played, even though it was mostly boasting.

"I'm tired uh' dat' dog barkin' all duh' time!" Antwaan exclaimed.

"Me too! I hear it all the way down the block. I know you be tired cause you live right next door."

"Yeah, and we can hear em' in the house yellin' too, so between the baby cryin' and duh' dog barkin' all night, I can't get no sleep. Dumb ol' stupid dog!"

"Yeah...stupid dog!"

"We should get ridda' dat' dog!"

"Whatchu' mean we?"

"I mean you and me. We friends, right? I ain't talkin' bout' nuthin' bad, we'll just run it off, you know, take it down duh' hill somewhere so we can't hear da' noise."

"I don't know. I ain't tryin' ta' get in no trouble. I ain't supposed ta' go down the hill."

"What, is you scared? That's it, you chicken!"

"No I'm not!"

That was the one thing no kid wanted to be called. No boy wanted to have his bravery questioned, so Herby reluctantly followed Antwaan to the back of Wexford Place and waited for

Teresa to put the dog out. It took about an hour and the boys were about to leave when Teresa appeared at the back door with the puppy in her arms. She put the bitch in the grass a few feet from the door and tied a string around her neck to keep her from wandering off. The puppy started whimpering immediately. Teresa was remorseless, ignoring the cries and quickly departing in order to start her evening activities. At first the boys played with the pup, after all, she was adorable as she wobbled about, testing her legs, sniffing the dirt, trees and bushes. That's where they first saw the Easy Bake oven, in the bushes, it was a toy that girls got for Christmas and birthdays at some point in their childhood. It had a light bulb inside and actually baked hand sized treats. This one was thrown away and missing the light bulb and batteries. The pink and blue plastic toy was dirty, dull, and weather beaten, but it was still detected by Antwaan.

    At the same time Teresa received the puppy, an acquaintance of her boyfriend became attracted to her. It was subtle at first but gradually she became aware of the attraction and the attention pleased her. Teresa had no intention of doing anything with the lady because she wasn't attracted to women. They first met when the lady came to hang out on the porch one evening. Her name was Tabitha and she was a twenty, three, year old pretty, dark skinned girl, with doe eyes, thick, long eyelashes and a little button nose accompanied her short, petite frame. Her silky sapphire hair draped her shoulders. She had a pretty smile with sparkling white teeth, and smiled often, especially when Teresa spread her legs. Tabitha would only glance at first but as she visited frequently, her glance turned into a stare since Teresa always sat with her legs open.

    It was late in the evening, approaching midnight, and Teresa drank too much alcohol. She felt light headed when Tabitha volunteered to help her to the bathroom. Teresa asked her boyfriend for assistance but he ignored her because he was angry that she was drunk. He continued to play Dominoes and smoke weed with his crew.

    "I'll help you baby," Tabitha smiled as she held Teresa's hand. Teresa looked up from her chair and returned her smile as she spread her legs as if to say, I know what you want. The alcohol made her loose and playful as she teased her admirer.

    "Come on baby, I got you," Tabitha continued.

"I gotta' pee! Help me to the bathroom, please. I can't make it, I'll be walkin' sideways. Whew, I'm feeling it, I musta' drank too much."

"Yeah, take yo' drunk ass inside! Out here embarrassing me. If you can't handle yo' liquor then don't drink so much stupid!" Her boyfriend yelled as he looked up from his Dominoes game to see Teresa stumbling, shuffling along, leaning on Tabitha for support.

"I ain't drr, dru, drunk," she stammered.

"That's all right. Don't listen to him. I'll take good care of you," Tabitha whispered.

"I bet you wu, wu, will," she giggled. "I see the way you been lookin' at me. You like Meeeee."

The women entered the house, then stumbled down the narrow hallway that led to the bathroom. The house was empty and this empowered Tabitha to act, so she gently massaged Teresa's butt when they entered the bathroom. She guided her to the toilet and burst with excitement when Teresa dropped her pants and squatted. No one paid any attention to their absence since they were high and drunk too, they didn't realize the ladies had been gone for over forty, five minutes. The women quietly returned to the porch, smiling. Teresa was walking on her own now, but Tabitha still held her hand, more from desire than assistance. When the ladies were in the bathroom Teresa passed out briefly, only to awaken and find Tabitha between her legs. She pushed her away initially, but Tabitha was strong and forced her face back between Teresa's legs. Now Teresa stopped struggling, seduced by the feeling since it was the first, time she experienced oral sex because her boyfriend didn't do that. Teresa always wondered what it felt like but she never imagined a lady would be the one to do it.

Since the other man was a woman, it was a while before her boyfriend understood Teresa was unfaithful. At first, he didn't care when Tabitha started to visit more frequently. He assumed Teresa had finally gotten a female friend. He was happy when Tabitha began to stay over till the early morning, after everyone else had gone, for he was attracted to her too, and only thought of his own lust when he decided to secretly pursue her. It was summer and now Tabitha wore miniskirts and t-shirts when she visited. He would brush against her, and touch her shoulders, and wrap his arm around her waist when he stood behind her, thrusting his pelvis against her. His fellas would laugh but Tabitha would squirm and wiggle free, to his disappointment. Teresa saw this and was unconcerned because Tabitha fulfilled her sexual desire. Each time they were together, it was three times so far, Tabitha stayed down there longer and longer, between her legs, purposefully seducing her, wanting Teresa to yearn for her touch when they were apart so that she wouldn't want to be without her. It was working, but now Teresa was unfulfilled having sex with her boyfriend when before she was happy. He noticed how she kept trying to guide his head between her legs, when before she didn't. He was older and more experienced than her so he knew something was different. Now, she always wanted more sex, when before once was enough, and on the occasions when he did comply it only intensified her desire. He had the feeling she would have sex all night if he was willing.

He would have never discovered the betrayal if not for his friends. They noticed the interaction between Teresa and Tabitha, since their actions were no longer subtle. Now the women openly gazed into each, others eyes and always sat close together, with Tabitha sitting on the floor between Teresa's legs as she sat in her chair, playing in Tabitha's hair. It wasn't unusual to her boyfriend because girls did this all the time when they were getting their hair braided, but she wasn't getting her hair braided. The ladies feed each other drinks, and blew blunt smoke into each, others mouth, closely, as their lips almost touched. There actions were intimate and his guys, along with some of their girlfriends, pointed this out to him so he could notice.

"What y'all talkin' bout' dey' like each other?"

"Looks that way to me man. Just watch how they act when they're together. You'll see when Tabitha get here. I been noticing it for a couple of weeks now."

"Well, I haven't been noticing nuthin."

"Cause' you too busy tryin' ta' get that ass."

Teresa's boyfriend laughed because he knew it was true, but still he lied and said, "Naw' man, we just friendly, she be sittin' on my lap and stuff," he smiled.

"And I know you like dat'. You just as bad as her. You don't even care, you be touchin' her right in front uh' yo' girl."

"Hey, if she can touch her then I can touch her too."

The men continued their conversation while Teresa got dressed for the evening. The baby was asleep and she was excited at the thought of Tabitha's arrival, but something was different. She didn't notice it at first but gradually realized her puppy wasn't barking, and she was pleased. It wasn't completely dark yet and she figured her dog was finally growing up. Now she felt remorseful, and since she was dressed for the evening, she decided to be nice and fill the puppies bowl with water. She opened the back door and to her surprise her dog was gone. She looked around, slowly, methodically like a detective, and eventually located the string she used to tie her puppy. It was near the hedges so she trailed the grass beneath them, believing her pup might have wandered under them. She figured she would hear the bitch's cries, but when she didn't, she called out to her.

"Oreo! Come here babe, where you at booby! Come on out baby!"

She continued calling out and searched the length of the bushes until she came upon the Easy Bake oven. She didn't think anything of it at first. She saw it for what it was, a discarded toy. It was dark now and she couldn't see clearly when she pushed the toy aside and noticed the weight. It seemed odd for the toy to be so heavy. She had one when she was a girl and knew they weren't supposed to be so heavy. She raised the toy with both hands and peered into the oven, but since Oreo was covered in black fur and only her belly was white, Teresa thought someone stuffed a black towel inside, so she dropped the toy in the grass causing the oven door to pop open, and she screamed as Oreo's lifeless body rolled out.

"Nooooooo! Oreooooooooo! They killed my dog! Those damn kids killed my dog!"

The men were in the front of the house on the porch and heard her screaming.

"What she yellin' bout' now. Yo' man, your girl always yellin' bout' something."

"I know she be gettin' on my nerves. She be tryin' ta' act all bad cause' she know I ain't on the lease. She always threatening to kick me out."

"That's cold man, that's messed up!"

Just then Teresa burst through the front door screaming. Herby and Antwaan were on the sidewalk playing and were surprised at the volume of her shriek. It sounded bloodthirsty to them like the women in the vampire movies. It made them nervous because they were certain the dog wouldn't be found so soon, but still why all the horror in her voice, after all, they only hide her puppy from her, and only closed the oven tight to muffle it's whimpering. The boys didn't know the pup suffocated. They didn't know they killed her.

"They killed my dog! They killed my dog! They killed my dog!"

Teresa's eyes were red from crying and she menacingly scowled at the boys, thrusting both hands at them she horrifyingly chanted.

"They killed my dog! They killed my dog! They killed my dog!"

"What you talkin' bout' girl!" her boyfriend finally interjected, but she didn't stop screaming until he grabbed her.

"They killed Oreo! They killed her! Dem' bad ass kids right dare! They did it! Dey' killed her!" she screamed and saw the confused look on his face.

"Go, look in the back, by the bushes, you'll see her, she's dead!" Teresa was overcome with grief and wept openly. It was an ugly cry, as tears soaked her distorted cheeks and twisted lips, passing the mucus that dribbled from her nostrils, enhancing her wails.

"I know they didn't!" he shouted at the boys and glared into their eyes, scaring them to death. Herby didn't wait for them to discover the body, he started running home immediately before her boyfriend went to look. It was a terrified run, faster than he'd ever moved before, he couldn't believe he was part of such a heinous thing. He was frightened, ashamed, and sad because he didn't want to be a puppy murderer. It was a hard lesson for him to learn but it served him well in life. From this point on he never went along with anyone if he wasn't in agreement, no one, nowhere, concerning his friends of course. He encountered peer pressure many times in his life and he always thought back to this moment, the moment he learned in life there are no, "Do overs." You can't reset the clock and start again, something's cannot be undone, there's no coming back from death. He ran straight to the porch and nervously sat on the steps. Pam was already there playing with one of her friends.

"What she screamin' bout' now?" she asked, sounding grown as her friend smiled. The little girl liked Pam because she was fresh, and all the kids were amazed at how Pam said things they wanted to, but wouldn't.

"What she screamin' bout' Herby?"

"I don't know?"

"Yes you do! Stop lyin!" Pam was an expert liar so she knew when her brother wasn't telling the truth.

"Then why she lookin' down here. Uh oh, here she come! She looks mad. I know y'all did sumthin'. Oh... did you see that, she popped Antwaan in the head!"

Herby didn't wait for her to reach their house before he ran inside to hide. Teresa was shouting as she approached, she had stopped crying, all her sadness was gone, her grieving was over, consumed by anger; rage was her catalyst now and as she drew near Pam could finally make out her words.

"You bastards killed my dog!" she screamed, and Pam's eyes widened with glee as her mouth flew open, with eyebrows arched and ears pointed she ran into the house. She couldn't believe her brother had done such a thing and it electrified her, because she loved mayhem and was jealous, knowing it was something she would have done. She couldn't believe the boldness of the act, it was coldhearted, and she didn't consider her brother to be that way. She had to find out what happened. She ran past her mother who was in a daze once again, sitting on the sofa staring at the T.V. while chewing crust ice from a cup, and into the kitchen to her sister.

"They killed her dog," she whispered.

"Who dog, what are you talking about?"

"Herby and Antwaan, they killed Teresa's dog."

"What, the puppy? How you know?"

"She's comin' here screamin' sayin' dey' did it, and Herby just ran upstairs scared, so he musta' done something, Imma' go and find out what happened."

There was a loud knock on the door accompanied by Teresa's shouts.

"Come out here you stinkin' devils! You come out here right now!" she screamed, awaking Ellen from the spell depression held on her. She slowly shuffled to the door, expressionless, and Teresa cursed her immediately, and she cursed her children saying they were part of the horrible crime. Ellen stood in the doorway, shoulders slumped, her demeanor withdrawn, she was confused and only said she didn't know what Teresa was talking about, and proclaimed her children innocent, but Teresa was adamant and the more Ellen denied, the angrier she became, pointing in Ellen's face now as she shouted. Baby Girl wanted her mother to push the lady off their porch, and tell her to leave, but Ellen was docile and quiet. Baby Girl couldn't bear to watch the argument any longer, seeing her mother berated was to sever, so she ran from the kitchen to the front of the house and slammed the door in Teresa's face.

    Teresa was not deterred. Someone was going to pay for the murder and she turned her attention to Antwaan. She saw her boyfriend return furious and knew he discovered the body. She tried to intervene when he began to chase Antwaan because even though she wanted the boy beaten, she was afraid her boyfriend might kill him. Antwaan learned from being smacked by surprise earlier, and anticipated being chased. He jumped off his bike before her boyfriend could grab him and did the zigzag run so effectively that he couldn't be caught, as he dodged, and dipped from side to side, to the point where her boyfriend tripped and stumbled over his own feet. His friends laughed as they watched the chase, and their conversation about infidelity was forgotten when Tabitha arrived amongst the fracas.

    Teresa stormed past them, running to Antwaan's house to confront his parents. It was the wrong thing to do because this couple wasn't docile, they were young too, in their mid-twenties, the same as Teresa and her boyfriend. As soon as Teresa started yelling and screaming at them, they pushed her from the porch and she tumbled to the ground. Antwaan's mother cursed her and kicked at her but Teresa was too swift and scrambled away. She was good at yelling but when it came to fighting, she was afraid. Her boyfriend saw this and stopped chasing Antwaan. He came to her aid but as soon as he reached her, he was confronted by Antwaan's father. The men started scraping immediately, wrestling and punching each other while his mother chased Teresa down the block. Teresa fled leaving her boyfriend to fend off both of them because Antwaan's parents jumped him, and methodically beat him until he fled down the block too.

    Baby Girl watched from her porch as Teresa returned with the cops. She was screaming again and felt empowered because the police where there. She led them into her home and Baby Girl assumed they were going to the backyard, the scene of the crime, causing her heart to race from panic. It seemed to take forever for them to emerge, when they did Teresa looked at Baby Girl's house, pointing while leading the officers up the street. Baby Girl was truly afraid now, and rushed into the house, running upstairs to be with her siblings.

"What's goin' on out there? We was watchin' from duh' winduh' and saw dem' fightin? That's good for her. Don't nobody like her anyway! She always yellin' and screamin' at somebody, an she jus' as bad as dem'. She need ta' be yellin' at herself!" Pam was excited, and the conversation was one sided with her doing all the talking. Herby was quiet, and miserable. There was no excitement for him because he was ashamed of following his friend against his will. Antwaan got the better of him by calling him names, but if he knew the outcome, he would have gladly endured the name calling. His thoughts were abruptly interrupted by a knock at the door.

"Who dat' Tee Tee?"

"It's the police," Baby Girl replied, trying to sound as calm as possible.

"What? For real?" Pam was astonished because the cops had never come to their house before. She looked at Herby nervously and decided to scare him.

"Oh my lord, my lord, dey' comin' for ya'. Dey' comin' for ya' Herby," she said in her best old lady voice, and looked sorrowfully at her brother, "You best ta' git' yo' thangs'…. You ready?"

"But I don't wanna' go!" Herby cried and shook uncontrollably. "I didn't mean ta' do it. It wasn't me it was Antwaan. It wasn't meeeee!" He slumped down into the corner below the window seal but Pam was just getting started as the knocking continued. Their mother wasn't answering the door even though you could see into the house from the screen.

"Come on Herby, we gotta' hide ya'," she said, pulling him up by the arm and pushing him toward the closet.

"Now you git' in there and we'll tell em' you ran away."

Herby was relieved and seemed perfectly willing to evade capture for he was terrified. Pam closed him inside the closet and stood in front of it with her back leaning against the door as she held her hands over her mouth to muffle her laughter.

"Now you jus' stay in there and I'll tell ya' when they're gone."

The police continued to knock but now the noise was accompanied by Teresa shouting.

"You seen um' go in there. You see the door is open so go on in there and get um!" she exclaimed, agitating the officers who banged even harder now since there was no door bell. As usual Baby Girl had to be the one to intervene. She knew things would only get worse if no one addressed the officers, so she descended the stairs and bravely opened the door to the policeman's surprise.

"Yes sir?"

"Das' her right dare!"

"Lady, I thought you said two boys did it."

"Well, it was her brother! Where's that murderer!" Teresa shouted at Baby Girl.

"Lady you stand over there and let us do our job, I ain't gonna' tell you again, I'll lock yo' ass up!"

"But they killed my dog!"

"That's what you say but you didn't see nothing, you don't know who did it, so let me do my job!"

Teresa was quiet now for the thought of going to jail frightened her. Her boyfriend approached just in time to hear the officer's comments and held her hand while gently putting his arm around her.

"Is your mother home?" the officer asked calmly.

"Mama! The police are here. They wanna' talk to you."

Ellen slowly shuffled to the door while mumbling to herself. The officer understood immediately when he saw her, and looked at his partner for confirmation, knowing that she wasn't correct mentally. Her hair was uncombed and her clothes were disheveled. Her gaze was unfocused as she looked at the officer's beard, transfixed on it, not making eye contact with him. Baby Girl was nervous because her mother's demeanor had declined considerably since Teresa was last there. Her appearance was raggedy to the point where Baby Girl thought they might take her away for being an unfit mother.

"Mam, are you okay?"

"Mmm hmm."

"She ain't okay, she crazy, just look at her!"

"I told you to shut up!"

The officer's partner stood in front of Teresa and her boyfriend and started talking to them, but Baby Girl couldn't hear what they were saying. She wished her mother didn't look so bad. In her fragile state the commotion caused Ellen's hands to tremble.

"She's not feeling well sir. I'm taking care of her," Baby Girl replied and held her hand, placing her four little fingers in Ellen's palm with her thumb touching the outside. The contact was unwanted and Ellen pulled away, never looking at her daughter, disturbed by being touched she slowly wiped her hand on her hip. The officer saw this and it saddened him, which was unusual because he was a sixteen, year veteran on the force and had seen many terrible things. He was hardened by the job, it caused him to be unforgiving, especially when criminals were insensitive and hateful towards their victims. He saw child neglect before but it was rare for him to see a child so composed and intelligent with a family that was dysfunctional. He knew questioning Ellen would be useless so he continued his interview with Baby Girl instead.

"Is your father home?"

"No sir. He doesn't live with us."

The officer knew the answer before he asked the question, still he had to be sure. He seldom softened but he liked Baby Girl since she reminded him of his daughter. He could sense her strength and fortitude.

"How old are you?"

"I'm eight."

"Who else lives here?"

"My brother and sister."

"How old are they?"

"My brother is five and my sister is six."

His understanding was complete. He was dealing with a dysfunctional family where there was no parental guidance, and the children were left to fend for themselves. Fortunately for them, the eldest daughter was the guardian, even though she was a child she seemed remarkably capable. The officer knew it was unfair to put such a burden on her, but he had seen worst situations and knew not to get emotional.

"Mam, this lady is saying that your son and another boy killed her dog. Do you know anything about that? Where's your son now?

Ellen didn't answer until Baby Girl tugged on her shirt sleeve.

"My boy didn't do nothing. I told her before. She came up

her an I already told her that my boy ain't do nothing."

"She lyin', well where he at den! Let's ask him!" Teresa screamed. "He's a murderer, he killed my dog!"

"I told you not to interfere again lady. That's it, were outta' here! And you don't want me to come back cause' I'll arrest the whole bunch of you. I been up here before and y'all always making noise," he said addressing Teresa directly, "And y'all got the neighbors complaining, well not tonight, if I come back I'm locking everybody up!" the officer scowled as he turned toward the crowd that had gathered, and stomped past Teresa with his partner trailing him down the block to their squad car.

"You ain't gettin' away wit' dis'. You think you can kill my dog and nothings gonna' happen? You just wait, if I see anyone of dem' damn kids in front of my house Imma' kick um'. Das' right, you heard me, an' you can call the cops, they'll find um' buried in a ditch somewhere!" Teresa screamed. She was furious and wanted revenge.

"Aw shut up booger lips! You ain't gonna' do nothing!" Pam yelled from the upstairs window and the crowd roared with laughter as Teresa burst into tears again. Her boyfriend frowned and pointed his finger at Pam as if it were a gun, then motioned like he pulled the trigger. Baby Girl slammed the door when she saw this and yelled upstairs to her siblings, "Y'all get out that window right now!"

The crowd dispersed as they reveled in the spectacle that unfolded. It was early in the evening and the neighbors knew they had the remainder of the night to endure, knowing anything could happen. It was a volatile situation when the party crew had arrived at Teresa's house, but she was still in morning and depressed by the death of her pup so the usual noise and merriment was absent from the nights' festivities. The tenants of Wexford Place were pleased because they would finally get an evening of rest since there was no barking dog, and no loud party to disturb them.

XI

Caught cheating

     A month passed since her puppy was killed and Teresa was still in mourning. The thought of her puppy suffering as it struggled to breath, suffocating in an Easy Bake oven, caused her to have sleepless nights. Sometimes she awoke crying and shouting, "No!" repeatedly. Her boyfriend was startled at first as he lay next to her, but since it happened frequently, he was accustomed to it by now and barely showed concern, in fact, on this particular sunrise her outburst annoyed him.
     "You havin' anutha' one uh' those dreams again!" he frowned, alarming her since he had always been consoling. She didn't know his anger was really from her waning sexual desire. Teresa didn't realize that he noticed she was emotionless and never climaxed, never initiated sex, and only submitted when his pleading became physical, which was about three times a month.
     "Why you mad… You know what dey' did ta' Oreo…. Dey' killed my dog…… Poor thang' was jus' a pup."
     Her boyfriend was silent and began rubbing his body against her back as she lay facing away from him.
     "See das' all you think about right dare'. Humpin' on me. You don't even care that I'm sad. Can't chu' see this thang' got me all upset. Can't chu' see I'm grievin'."
     "Psssst!" her boyfriend replied, causing Teresa to roll over so quickly it surprised him. She was angry now and didn't care if he wanted her. She hit him on his arms, chest and head as she struggled to get on top of him, hindered by the tangled bed sheets. Once upon him she sat tall and tried to strangle him, but her boyfriend was strong and shifted his weight, kicked his legs, and bounced her off his stomach. Once free he quickly subdued her because he was still aroused and desired sex, and was driven by lust as he ripped her panties off. He grew angrier the more she struggled, but the more she fought the more aroused he became until he needed to release his frustration. He couldn't wait any longer

and wrapped his hands around her neck just as she had done to him. He wanted her to stop fighting so he slowly applied pressure, in increments, suffocating her gradually while her punches grew weaker. As Teresa gasped for air, she grew terrified by the glare in his eyes. She was afraid to die and knew how to make him stop choking her. She slowly spread her legs while laying still, so he could enter.

A month had passed since Herby and Antwaan killed Teresa's puppy. It was actually manslaughter, it was an accident because they really didn't want the pup to die, they just wanted to stop it from barking all night, every night. Herby couldn't sleep and often burst from slumber screaming and crying. Baby Girl was always consoling and would care for her brother even though he was five, and not a baby, she held him until he was calm. He always cried out the same thing.

"No! I didn't mean a do it!"

He lowered his voice as she rocked him in her arms and looked into her eyes as he spoke, trying to make her understand that he was still a good boy.

"I didn't mean a do it Tee Tee," he said as tears trickled down his chubby cheeks.

"I know you didn't...."

Baby Girl knew how to sooth her brother because she cared for him as an infant and was compassionate but Pam was not. Since she was the middle child and insane, Pam grew jealous of the attention Herby was getting. When at first, she was considerate, now she was irritated by his nightmares.

"You still havin' bad dreams cause' you a killa'...." she scowled.

"No I'm not! I didn't mean a do it! It was an ax uh' dent! It wasn't my fault!"

Just when Baby Girl had him calm, Pam's words excited him, causing him to cry out once again. Pam smiled in her bed with her back turned away from her siblings, reveling in the pain she Instigated.

"Don't listen to her. I know you didn't mean to do it. I know you're good, and nice, and sweet," Baby Girl said with a smile, as she softly touched his nose.

"No he ain't! He a killa!"

"No I'm not! It wasn't my fault!" Herby shouted. He was

out of control now and struggled with Baby Girl to get to Pam.

"You shut your mouth Pam and mind your business!"

Baby Girl was upset because she knew her sister enjoyed causing trouble. Pam was a sociopath so whenever things were going well, she had to be disruptive. She didn't care about the circumstances or the people involved, family or not.

"No! He botherin' me! Always wakin' me up wit' duh' screamin' an cryin' …I'm sick of it!"

"He's your brother. You're supposed to take care of him, not upset him!"

"I don't care if he's my brother, he a killa!"

"Tee Tee make her stop! Make her stop sayin' dat!"

Herby yelled, fiercely kicking his feet, struggling to free himself from Baby Girl's grip in order to pounce on his sister. The death of the puppy was an accident but if he reached Pam, her death would be premeditated because Herby wanted to kill her. Her words flamed his anger and consumed his thoughts until only murder remained. Pam saw this and laughed outright now as she pointed at Herby and mocked him.

"Let him go! Little baby, you ain't gonna' do nuthin! Let him go Tee Tee!"

Herby cried and squirmed, trying to free himself as he growled like a wolf. The excitement awoke Candace so she sat up in her bed while clapping, screeching and drooling. She thought it was fun because she was a baby and wanted to add to the chaos, therefore, she made as much noise as possible while crawling about the bed, attempting to stand.

"Y'all betta' stop all dat' noise in dare! Fo' I come in dare'n whip all uh' y'all!" their mother screamed.

Ellen was tired, depressed, and wanted to be free of her children, but since she could not, she ignored them, usually, until they upset her. Baby Girl wanted to take control of the chaos. She knew her mother was sick because her mind was fragile. She didn't want her condition to worsen so she snatched Herby from the bed and dragged him out the room. She took him downstairs to the kitchen. Pam was having fun and wasn't about to let them get away that easy so she followed them, leaving Candace in the room unattended.

"Where y'all think y'all goin'…." Pam snickered as she burst into the kitchen.

"You better get back upstairs. You ain't nothing but the devil. You can't even leave well enough alone."

"Yeah, you ain't nuthin' but duh' devil," Herby chimed in. He was feeling better now because Baby Girl gave him a piece of ice to suck on.

"You shut up puppy killa!"

"I aint' no puppy killa, das' why you duh' devil!"

Herby stopped crying and noticed how calling his sister a devil upset her so naturally he continued his taunts.

"Puppy killa!"

"Devil!"

"Puppy killa!"

"Devil!"

The chaos returned as the children shouted at one another, unaware that Candace had crawled to the edge of the bed and decided to follow them downstairs since she heard their voices and wanted to take part in the mayhem. She usually slid off the bed feet first but this time she landed awkward, twisting her foot, causing her to cry out immediately.

"Pam, you know you can't leave Candace up there by herself, you crazy?" Baby Girl said when she heard Candace.

"Yeah, you crazy?"

"I forgot she was up there!"

Their mother heard her toddler whimpering and grew furious. Her dark smelly room was next to the children's and she couldn't understand why Baby Girl didn't stop Candace from crying.

"Tina! Where you at? Don't chu' hear yo' sista' cryin!"

"See, now you upset mama. I told you to be quiet, that's why I took him down here, but noooo.... you gotta' follow behind us and now Candace is crying!"

"I'm not going up there and leave you two together so you gotta' go."

"I don't wanna' go, mama's awake now and she stink."

"I'll go Tee Tee."

"No Herby she gotta' go. Pam, stop complaining before I pop you!"

Pam angrily stomped upstairs and returned to their room to see what happened to Candace. She passed her mother's room and was insulted.

"Whatchu' dun' did now you little crab!" Her mother yelled, "I know it was you ya' little fat liar! It's always you. You always startin' trouble. I shoulda' neva' had you!"

Pam was usually numb to her mother's words but this time she was hurt by them. She could detect the hate in her mother's voice and it saddened her. Since she was crazy, Pam was compelled to hurt someone whenever she was hurt, unfortunately Candace was the only one around she could inflict pain upon, so when she reached her baby sister, she immediately smacked her in the head.

"You betta' shut up all dat' noise stupid!" she yelled.

Candace was more shocked than hurt. She couldn't understand how her two sisters acted so differently. One was kind and the other was mean, forcing her to act differently too, depending on which sister she was interacting with. She knew with Pam she had to be tough, while with Baby Girl she could be herself, laughing and playing to her hearts' desire.

It was evening now and Teresa was still shocked from being raped. She was frightened too because she didn't know if her boyfriend would do it again. She observed no remorse in his words and actions afterward, in fact, he was still angry, not furious like before because he was satisfied sexually, but she noticed that he wasn't satisfied mentally.

"You betta' stop playin' wit' me cause I ain't no play thang'....and I ain't no little boy sniffin' round' dat' you think you can string along......I'm a grown ass man and you betta' start respectin' me.....I got needs....You my woman so you supposed ta' take care uh' dat'.....It's your duty as my woman ta' make sure I'm good...." he said, trying to engage her in conversation, pausing after each sentence to let her speak, only to be met with silence. She quietly lay on the bed staring at the ceiling, hoping he would leave her alone. He grew melancholy when she wouldn't look at him, but he was still unapologetic as he left the room and went downstairs to the kitchen.

He wanted to know why Teresa wasn't aroused by him since he had always satisfied her in the past. He didn't believe her abstinence was a result of Oreo's death, since it began prior to that. He thought about it all day, not getting high, not getting drunk, he wanted to think clearly, he wanted to be sure. He studied the calendar on the wall to help his memory. As he ran his fingers backward on the days and numbers, he realized Teresa's sexual desire gradually diminished soon after that fateful night when Tabitha helped her to the bathroom, when she was intoxicated. He studied it until, he was sure. He looked at the date and the days that followed to analyze her movements. His friends told him they noticed the ladies' demeanor, and he observed how they were always together when Tabitha visited. At first, he was unconcerned because he knew Teresa wasn't attracted to girls, but when he thought deeply, scenes of the women playing in each, others hair, as they sat between one another, and the delicate way they interacted, flashed in his mind forcing him to confront the truth, compelling him to understand the women never acted this way before that deceitful night, now his simmering anger grew steadily.

As he sat downstairs at the kitchen table, he heard Teresa moving about and figured she was getting their son ready for bed. The baby was six months old, able to sit up, and starting to crawl. It was Teresa's normal routine at this time to bath him and change his pamper, so her boyfriend waited anxiously for her to finish, because he wanted her to come downstairs so he could confront her. He knew she would lie therefore he decided to call Tabitha and invite her over. The only way he could accurately gauge their reactions and discover the truth was to have them both present.

A month had passed since Teresa's puppy was killed and Tabitha was in love. She only realized it when they were apart. She was present that horrible night when Teresa found the pup, and hadn't seen her since, and was told it was because of the murder but she felt Teresa's boyfriend was somehow to blame. She knew he liked her and didn't want her to be with Teresa unless he could have her too. At first Tabitha thought about having a threesome just to have sex with Teresa, but when the opportunity came to be alone with her beloved, she was pleased. Tabitha slept with men before but preferred women. Her first experience with a girl occurred in high school when a class mate seduced her, since then, she found sex with men awkward, they were selfish lovers and she never climaxed, but she did with women, so she decided to only be with ladies. It was a recent decision, with Teresa, it was Tabitha's first time being the seducer, prior to that, she had always been the one seduced.

To Tabitha's surprise the phone rang and Teresa's boyfriend greeted her. He told her to come over and she was happy to be invited. Her heart beat swiftly from the thought of seeing her beloved. She reminisced about their last encounter, trying to experience the moment again to no avail. She needed to see Teresa to satisfy her desire. It didn't occur to Tabitha that her infatuation would not be there. She didn't think about Teresa's boyfriend being alone, she only concentrated on seeing her lover. Her desire guided her, dismissing her better judgment, overriding her senses, rendering her helpless and vulnerable, deactivating her brain so it couldn't protect her with logical thought. She moved like a merry zombie as she systematically selected an outfit to wear. Every motion excited her since she knew all her actions were leading up to their reunion. She imagined how Teresa looked, although it was only thirty days, it seemed longer because she had no picture to gaze upon.

    Teresa's boyfriend needed to have the women together to be sure. He knew if he confronted them in person, he could tell by their reaction if they were lying, if his suspicions were true, so he didn't tell Teresa that Tabitha was coming when she entered the kitchen and walked to the refrigerator to get a beer. She turned on the radio, turned up the volume and bopped her head in rhythm with the music. Teresa was trying to forget the past twelve hours. It was the worst half a day she had ever experienced. Being raped made her feel helpless. She was mentally drained, she was afraid and unaccustomed to fear, so she decided to bury her emotions. She was eager to forget her nightmare, hoping that by ignoring the attack it would go away and never return. It was a foolish thought but Teresa was depressed and didn't want to face reality. She sat in the chair across from her boyfriend at the small table, not making eye contact with him she began preparing her blunt for the marijuana she was about to roll. Her boyfriend didn't mind being ignored because he knew Tabitha was coming so he decided to suppress his anger until she arrived.

    It was night time and Baby Girl had spent the day playing with her siblings. They stayed on the porch and around the house. They hadn't ventured down the block since the murder. The children were still afraid even though it happened a month ago. She remembered the gun sign Teresa's boyfriend made with his hand that fateful night. She knew he was in a gang and wanted to be careful not to provoke him. She was protective of her siblings but it was easy because they had no desire to go down the block. She was reading a book to them, their favorite, "Frog and Toad Go Swimming," when she heard a lady screaming. She looked out the window and saw Teresa running from her boyfriend. Her shirt was ripped and hair disheveled as if she were fighting. She was crying as she ran up the street toward Baby Girls' house.

"What's goin' on out dare?"

"It's Teresa. She running from her boyfriend and screaming."

"What! Move... I gotta' see dis!"

Pam jumped from her bed and crowded Baby Girl at the window to witness the spectacle. Herby was still nervous, remorseful, and couldn't bear any drama so he stayed in bed to avoid watching the fracas.

"No Eddie!" Teresa screamed as she ran, merely to be snatched by her hair and restrained by her boyfriend.

"Eddie! It wasn't my fault! I was drunk! I didn't know what was happening! I passed out and the next thang' I know she on top uh' me!"

"You think I'm a fool. Y'all been sneakin' round' all this time! Laughing at me! I'll give you something to laugh at!" Eddie yelled as he slapped Teresa in her head and face. She tried to fend him off the best she could but she was no match for his precise blows. The girls looked from their window in amazement with Pam being more animated.

"Oh.... you see dat'. He beatin' her bad. Look.... she dun' fell and he still hittin' her. Oooooh' she tryin' ta' crawl away. Ooooh' he kicked her! She really cryin' now. Herby you missin' it. Teresa getting' her butt whooped. Don't chu' wanna' see?"

Herby sat quietly and began rocking slowly while the assault continued.

"You jus' scared ta' look das' all. They ain't thinking bout' you. I wonder what happened. That's good for her cause' she always mean and yelling. I wonder what she did. I know she did sumthin' cause' he wouldn't be hittin' her like dat'. She had ta' do sumthin' .... right Tee Tee."

"Well he sure isn't beating her for nothing," Baby Girl replied.

When Tabitha arrived, Teresa was surprised to see her. Eddie noticed the expression on her face and took it as an admission of guilt. He witnessed Tabitha burst with adoration as she could barely contain her love. Underestimating her affection and unable to control it, Tabitha startled herself by moving so quickly, clumsily rushing toward Teresa who was still sitting. Now Teresa's expression changed from shock to fear when she noticed Tabitha was unconcerned that Eddie was present, and revealed her emotions freely while holding Teresa entirely too long when they embraced.

"You sleepin' wit' her!" Eddie screamed as he frowned at the women. Only then did Tabitha release her beloved. She looked at Teresa with a puzzled expression, then looked at Eddie and could tell he knew what was in her heart. It was impossible to conceal her love because it danced in her eyes. She said nothing and backed away from her beloved slowly, returning her gaze and fixing it on her face only to be betrayed when Teresa nervously looked away, shifting her eyes to Eddie, but she couldn't endure his scowl and shifted her eyes back to Tabitha who seemed genuinely hurt.

"What chu' talkin' bout' Eddie! Why you actin' crazy!" Teresa yelled, franticly trying to change Tabitha's demeanor with her words, but the scene grew worst, and Teresa was mortified when Tabitha started to cry.

"Why she cryin' den!"

"Baby, I don't know……"

"What she cryin' fo' den' if y'all ain't doin' nuthin!"

"Baby I don't know. We ain't do nuthin.' We ain't messin' round. You must be crazy cause das' nasty and I don't do dat!"

Now Tabitha howled as her tears flowed, cascading past her lips, landing on her chest, causing her pain as a result of her love being denied.

"I don't know why she crying. We ain't do nuthin' I swear!"

It was too late for words. The women's actions convinced Eddie that he was right, but instead of being relieved at knowing the truth, his rage caught him off guard as the sight of the women having sex, laughing at him, flashed in his mind.

"You get outta' my house!" he shouted, and pushed Tabitha with force against the cabinets, causing her to break some dishes, startling Teresa. She abruptly jumped from her chair.

"Eddie stop! Leaver alone!"

"I bet you'd like that huh! I bet you'd like to be alone wit' her huh!"

Eddie moved closer to attack Tabitha again but Teresa blocked his path only to be knocked to the floor. She held onto his legs and screamed, "Run Tabby…. Get outta' here!"

Now Tabitha was finally afraid and rushed past Eddie to escape through the rear door.

"You protectin' her you dirty hoe! I'll show you what you git' fur' runnin' round' behind my back!" he yelled as he struck her repeatedly, causing her to release his legs and escape through the rear door too, but her retreat was accompanied by slaps and punches as she stumbled from being pushed mercilessly.

"Tee Tee you see dat! Here dey' come!" Pam was ecstatic because the beating had reached their house, and the sisters view was clear as they saw and heard everything. Eddie was too busy assaulting Teresa to notice them but just as she ran past their house, Teresa glanced up at the girls' window only to be met with the joyous smirk that Pam displayed when she rolled her eyes, scrunched her lips, and pocked her chin out while moving her head from side to side. It gave her so much pleasure to know that Teresa witnessed her teasing, and saw that she was evil, insensitive, and unremorseful to her suffering. Pam's revenge was complete, she felt vindicated and believed Teresa deserved it, even though it was the worst time to taunt her, which made it even more enjoyable.

The neighbors were upset and tired of the couple's endless disturbances, tonight's commotion being the worst, so one of them called the police.

"You hear dat! It's duh' cops! Dey' comin! You hear the sirens, you see the flashing lights, duh' cops is comin!" Pam shouted as she jumped up and down, ecstatic, unable to contain her emotions.

"It's a lot of um' look…. one, two, three, four cars…there's four cars Tee Tee!"

"I see, I'm right here."

"Das' good for dem'. Dey' always makin' noise….and she wanna' come and tell us ta' be quiet! Shoot, she must be crazy!"

Baby Girl smiled because it was funny to hear her crazy sister say someone else was crazy.

"Oh… dey' got him now, look…. dey' lockin' him up! Oh, you see dem' slam him on duh' car like dat! That's messed up, dem' cops is mean!"

Eddie was still chasing and hitting Teresa when the police arrived. He was oblivious to them, consumed by rage from her betrayal. They witnessed his actions and jumped on him, first two policemen, then four, as they held him down, kneeling on his back and neck while handcuffing him. He continued to struggle even though he was subdued, that's when he was slammed on the hood of the patrol car by the same officer who was present when the puppy was killed. He was the one who warned them to leave Baby Girl's house or they would be arrested, so he knew the couple was a nuisance and this angered him.

After throwing Eddie in the car the police only spoke to Teresa briefly before leaving. They asked her if she wanted to go to the hospital but she declined. She had a bloody nose, black eye, cuts on her arms and elbows, scrapes on her knees, her clothes were torn, dirty, and she only wore one flip flop since the other was lost during the scuffle. Now Pam laughed outright and started to yell but was hampered by Baby Girl who knew she was going to say something terrible, so she held her mouth.

"You better shut up. You want her to come up here after the cops leave. I don't want no trouble. It's been quiet and I want to keep it that way."

"Lemme' go," Pam mumbled, "I ain't gonna' say nuthin."

"You better not. I'm not playing with you."

"I'm not gonna' say nuthin."

"Okay……I'm letting go…you better be quiet," Baby Girl said and removed her hands from Pam's mouth.

Pam slowly backed away from the window but she couldn't contain her desire to taunt Teresa, and shouted, "Booger lips! That's good for you!" then ran out the room. Baby Girl was too upset to chase her and sat on the bed with Herby who was happy to have the company, and glad the fighting was over.

Two days later Teresa was gone. She wasn't forced to leave but voluntarily decided to go. Her man, the father of her child, was locked up, even though she went to the police station and dropped the charges they still held him for resisting arrest, and said they would charge him with assaulting her too because the officers witnessed it. Now she was alone for the first time in her life and couldn't bare being around her neighbors after such an embarrassing scene. She saw Pam tease her and knew some of the neighbors would do the same, especially Antwaan's parents since they lived next door, and had already fought.

The moving truck arrived at daybreak, then three workers spent the morning loading her furniture and belongings. It only took a few hours since she didn't have much. By 10am they were gone. Baby Girl saw them drive away because she was an early riser. Then a half an hour later Teresa emerged and got into a taxi with her son, carrying a backpack and two suit cases. She wore sun glasses to cover her black eye. The swelling had gone, but it was darker now with red scars below the eye lid. She was exhausted from the stress of living on Wexford Place, even though it was only seven months, and happy to be leaving. As the taxi passed Baby Girl's house Teresa looked up at the window and saw her. She promptly stuck her middle finger up, high in the air, out the cab window, then sunk into her seat, disgusted. Baby Girl was shocked at first, but then she realized Teresa was like her evil sister Pam, and soon forgot her parting gesture. She smiled because now she wouldn't have to worry about going down the block, or the couple's retribution.

XII

SHE A HOE!

Cleopatra was a beautiful bronze model, with manicured nails, and lush lips that seemed as if they were molded to fit the contours of her shapely cheeks. Her narrow eyes revealed her bloodline from the south pacific, mesmerizing all who looked into them, causing people to do her bidding for they had never seen someone her complexion with eyes shaped like that. Such an exotic mixture was rare, and Baby Girl adored her. Her thick, auburn, eyebrows were pointed on the ends with a natural arch that accompanied her petite forehead, which supported her crown, which secured her golden brown, curly, mane. Cleo, as she was called, cut and styled her locks often since they grew quickly, but currently she let them drape her shoulders because men were attracted to this look, and she wanted to keep them happy since she was a whore.

To be accurate, she was a prostitute, and her present lifestyle was an unwanted business decision. She came upon the profession gradually as a way to survive, as a way to have money to live financially independent, free from the burden of debt, free from the burden of marrying for money, in fact, she had extra money after her bills were paid and this enabled her to travel as she pleased, live where she chose, and move whenever she desired. There was still the matter of having sex with strangers. So many men at first, but now, having been in the profession for seven years, she had regular customers.

The hardest part of being a prostitute for Cleopatra was discretion. She lived a double life so secrecy was necessary since she entertained men at home, solely, because it was a controlled environment. Her neighbors eventually became suspicious as there was no way to explain all the men. She ran out of uncles, cousins, and nephews, which she called her clients, and tried to space their visits between morning, noon, and evening, but eventually some disturbance would happen and she would move. The longest she lived at one location was eleven months, that is until she moved next to Baby Girl on Wexford Place.

Given that she never dated her tricks, the second hardest part of being a prostitute was avoiding stalkers and psychopaths, which included women. Sometimes jealous wives and girlfriends would follow their men to her home, confronting her instead of them, enraged, crying, screaming, and trying to claw her silky skin. One lady even pulled a razor and tried to slice her exquisite face, but luckily Cleo instinctively lowered her head and received a cut on her scalp instead. It was a dangerous tightrope she lived because someone would eventually come around unannounced, harassing her, or worse, falling in love.

She was good at disappearing. She was an actress and enjoyed reestablishing herself in new locations. She imitated an undercover agent as she reserved an escape plan, keeping one suitcase packed with clothes and money, to travel light without notice. Cleo kept cash but her checking account was her real ally. She wasn't going to keep all her money in the house for fear of getting robbed, or a fire occurring, and she wasn't about to risk losing her life savings. Being twenty, four, she was proud of the twenty, seven thousand dollars she accumulated, and used a checking account because she could withdraw money anytime, unlike a savings account where she would be penalized. She never kept more than one hundred dollars in cash, which is equivalent to $430 dollars today, and wrote checks for everything, but didn't except them from her Johns.

Credit cards weren't widely used in 1977, and there were no Debit cards, but she was confident about her retirement if she continued saving. Her goal was to retire at thirty, sooner if possible because she was tired of being a hooker. To alleviate her unhappiness, every year Cleo took several vacations to the Caribbean, and West Indies, where she was wealthier because U.S. currency was superior on certain islands. She lived like a queen abroad and dreaded each time she had to return to the states. Once she saved enough money to retire, it was definitely going to be in some far away land where she could live comfortably.

Cleopatra was from San Diego, California; the daughter of poor parents who migrated across the country to Cincinnati, Ohio, in search of a better life. Her father was Japanese and her mother was Ethiopian. Like Baby Girl she was born an old soul, and absorbed knowledge, being a child that was mature beyond her years. She discovered the cruelty of the world at an early age when her father was killed due to street violence and her mother fell victim to drug addiction, leaving her unsupervised, uncared for, and alone to fend for herself. She was an only child, unlike Baby Girl who had to look after her younger siblings, so she learned quickly to use her beauty to her advantage. She discovered that people were naturally drawn to her so if she was friendly, she could ask them for little things like food, or spare change. They would give it to her because she chose older adults to play with, usually grandmothers or grandfathers. She'd stare into their eyes gleefully, and when they were captivated, she'd act as though she was their child, and dance around their legs like when their children were learning to walk. This usually brought out their paternal instincts. She would run from people that wanted to abduct her, when they discovered she was alone. During this crucial time in her life Cleopatra found her angel.

  She was six when Mother Grant, as she was known in the community, being an elder member of Little Friendship Baptist church, took her into her home against the protest of the congregation because Mother Grant had taken in a child before, only to have the girl steal from her and run away, they felt she was too nice and being preyed upon once again. Their opinions changed once she brought Cleopatra to church for the first time. The sight of this exotic child enamored everyone as she glided to the front of the church, guided by Mother Grant, who instructed her to sit in the second row behind the rest of the church Mothers who wore white uniforms and were considered prime council. Now Cleopatra finally had a stable environment and flourished. She made her first escape at this time, leaving her biological mother who barely noticed she was gone, and never looked for her, being content with one less mouth to feed.

  Cleopatra was taught all the aspects of being a lady; from attire, to posture, homemaking, cooking, cleaning, and proper hygiene. Even though she was sociable, she was taught how to address people in conversation. Cleo had never attended school regularly, so at first it was difficult to adapt, but after time she excelled in class, and proudly showed Mother Grant her grades since she knew it would make her happy. She felt being a good person and performing well in school was the least she could do to show her appreciation. Her favorite subject was math, she liked the certainty of it, facts comforted her, knowing if the numbers were correct then the problem would be solved, caused her to apply this truth to her finances when she began accumulating money.

Mother Grant had three children, two daughters and a son, but they were grown and rarely visited, leaving her sad and alone until Cleopatra came into her life. Now she finally had someone to love, given that it was suppressed for so long, she felt relieved to release it, she felt needed once again. Until meeting Cleo, she was lost and unsure. She knew she had a purpose in life but was unable to be charitable like she desired. Of course, giving tithes to the church, which was ten percent of your earnings, and donating to charity, was something, but caring for someone and saving a life was more rewarding to her. She spoiled Cleo with each coming year, unable to resist buying her toys, clothes, and little shiny trinkets to decorate her hair, neck, and wrist. Cleo was astute and aware of the jealousy her guardian caused by making her regal and luxurious, so she always behaved accordingly, only saying and doing nice things, being gracious made her acceptance possible.

Her life was proceeding well until Mother Grant became sick. The diagnosis was breast Cancer and because it was discovered in the latter stages, there was nothing the physicians could do, only make her comfortable, giving her about a year to live. Cleo was sixteen now, captivatingly beautiful, and rendered men speechless upon seeing her. They fumbled their words, or smiled too broadly, which always upset their wives. She had a growth spurt and was five feet ten inches now, taking after her father who was a tall man. During this time, she stayed out of school to look after Mother Grant who always protested, but was grateful for the help. When the cancer became too severe and rendered her bedridden, the church mothers took over caring for her in the day, so Cleo could continue classes. She would resume caring for Mother Grant after school, foregoing socializing with classmates, or dating the school boys who clamored for her attention. She loved her guardian and wanted to show her appreciation by caring for her just like she had been cared for. Towards the end of Mother Grant's life, her eldest daughter visited, only to be met with this exquisite caretaker whom she thought was hired by the church, but when she learned her mother had accepted the role of guardian once again, she was upset and confronted Cleopatra.

"How you know my mama? I thought you was hired by the church for homecare."

"She got me when I was six."

"What you mean got you? Don't tell me you another one of those runaways. Lawd' she keep bringing these kids in here like stray dogs. How old are you now?"

"I'm sixteen and I ain't no stray dog!"

"My mama been taking care of you for ten years? I can't believe this! I didn't know nothing bout' that! Wait till' I tell my sister and brother you staying here, taking advantage of our mama, we gonna' kick your ass out!"

"I'm not taking advantage of her. She's my mother now cause' my real mama didn't want me, and I'm her daughter cause' her real children don't want her…. and we're gonna' keep living like this till' she die and there ain't nothing you can do about it! You would have known about me if you ever visited, but you haven't been around in ten years. Where you been? Didn't you wanna' know how she was doing? She's an old woman…. wasn't you concerned?!"

Mother Grant's daughter didn't want to tell Cleo that she spent the last five years in prison, the result of running off with a conman who left her to take the blame for a crime he committed, so she decided to wait until her mother died to pursue the eviction, after all, she saw how frail her mother had become and believed the doctor's timeframe to be accurate, therefore, she was content to wait a few months to reap the benefits of her mother's wealth.

As I said before, the longest Cleopatra stayed at a location was her current residence on Wexford Place, up the street from Baby Girl, living there for over two years. The first three months Cleo lived undetected because it was cold and people stayed indoors, but when spring arrived Baby Girl noticed the exotic beauty since she regularly relaxed in her lounge chair on the grassy knoll next to her house. It was a beautiful setting, however, none of the kids played in that area given that most of the excitement occurred down the block in the valley. Cleo liked to read in the afternoon and noticed the little girl who sat on the porch after school, reading also. She observed how Baby Girl seemed more mature than the other kids as she kept to herself, enthralled in whatever book she was reading while the rest of the children played. She often saw Baby Girl smile and laugh as she read, which peaked her curiosity since she wasn't accustomed to seeing a child voluntarily reading, especially if it was for amusement and not a school assignment. When she witnessed her reading on the weekends, she became enamored with the little princess and decided to talk to her.

"Hey my dear! I see you like reading!" she called out one spring Sunday morning. Baby Girl didn't hear her at first, but on the third call she looked up from her book and realized the beauty was addressing her.

"Are you talking to me miss?"

"Yes, I was wondering what you were reading?"

"It's a short story by Edgar Allen Poe called, The Raven."

"Edgar Allen Poe? What do you know about him? That's literature for Middle School. What grade are you in dear?"

"I'm in the second grade but he's my teacher's favorite author so I wanted to see what made his stories so interesting."

"Well good for you. So, what do you think?"

"I like it. It rhymes. The whole story, like a poem, but I never read a poem this long. Well…. it's not really a poem it's a short story, and yet, he still finds a way to make it rhyme. It's supposed to be scary but it's just creepy to me. I like the way the bird keeps returning, causing the man to go insane."

"So just because your teacher likes him you decided to read his work."

"Sort of, Mrs. Wells, that's my teacher, she mentioned it was one of her favorite stories so I decided to read it."

"You must be smart because that's literature reserved for older students."

She liked the way Cleopatra said, literature. She sounded like a teacher, since Baby Girl never heard an adult say that word outside of school. They usually said, books.

"You must really like Mrs. Wells."

Baby Girl smiled bashfully because Cleo was right. Mrs. Wells was her idol and she wanted to impress her.

When she gazed upon the model, she was drawn to her since she had never met a lady so beautiful and smart. She was filled with many questions but wasn't accustomed to talking to strangers so she stayed quiet and only spoke to Cleo when she addressed her, even though she desired to know her life story. She did ask Cleo if she had any children and was surprised when she said no.

Eventually she made her way to the grassy knoll. She was coaxed by Cleopatra of course, who enticed her with kind words and freshly baked cookies. Once together the two spent hours in conversation while reading various books that she possessed. Prior to their meetings, Baby Girl never met an adult, besides teachers, that collected books. She learned Cleo's goal was to create a library with her favorite novels all arranged in alphabetical order. Before reading something new she would say, "You're not going to have this book on your reading list at school," then Cleopatra began reading the tale of the lovelorn couple in Harlem, in the 1920's. The lady was a butter complexioned dancer at The Cotton Club. Her soul mate was a tall, chocolate complexioned, saxophone player in the band, and their secret love was doomed from the beginning. It was a sordid tale filled with excitement, mayhem and mystery. Cleo would show her a picture of the author first, usually someone from the Harlem Renaissance, and then begin reading the first page and let her read the second, they continued this way, alternating pages, until the end. Cleo was impressed with Baby Girl's reading skills. Every so often she would pause to ask the definition of a word, aside from that, she smoothly finished each page while emphasizing the excitement, or sadness in the story, causing Cleopatra to smile. The pair initially bonded over their love of reading, but gradually, some afternoons they didn't read at all, they just laid on a blanket and stared at the sky, imagining the clouds were their creation and naming them. Baby Girl loved this because she was encouraged to use her creativity.

About a year into their relationship Cleopatra had quietly settled into the neighborhood and was unaware she had a spy. Her new little friend would gaze out the window in the cold months, transfixed on Cleo's house. She witnessed her male companions visiting, frequently. The various men did peak Baby Girls' curiosity but not to the extent of worry, it was interesting though, as she noticed one man in particular visiting at least three times a week. He was an older man and she thought maybe he was related to Cleo. Convincing herself of this over time, she relaxed, thinking how nice it must be to have a family member check on you to make sure you're okay.

On this particular evening Pam ran into the kitchen, excitedly telling her siblings that the police were outside.

"The Cops is outside!" she yelled, startling Baby Girl, Herby and Candace.

"Dey' is?" Herby replied, sharing Pam's enthusiasm.

"Yeah, dey' sittin' in front uh' dat' pretty lady's house."

"Who? Cleopatra?" Baby Girl asked, and her siblings giggled at the sound of this exotic name.

"What kind uh' name is dat!?"

"Yeah…. what kind uh' name is it?" Herby said, imitating Pam.

"Oh be quiet. You don't know anything!" Baby Girl shouted, then she went to the window to see for herself. She saw a police car in front of Cleo's house and began to worry. She wondered if her infatuation was in trouble. She couldn't imagine anything unlawful occurring and noticed about an hour later the car was gone. She never saw the officer but was curious to know his identity, just in case she recognized him.

Ellen shuffled into the kitchen, dragging her feet in her dirty, worn, stinky grey slippers. She ignored her children while retrieving a tray of ice from the freezer, mumbling softly, incoherently to herself. Her children watched quietly as she filled a cup with ice, then Pam decided to wake her from her trance.

"Mama! You missed it mama! The Cops was outside!"

Ellen frowned, and stared into her cup, annoyed that she was being addressed.

"Mama didja' hear me! The cops was outside!"

Baby Girl stood in the kitchen doorway now and saw her mother gradually awaken. At first, Ellen's frown turned to confusion as Pam repeated her statement. Then finally a break thru, as a result of the constant badgering, Ellen spoke.

"What you done did now?"

"I didn't do nothing. Dey' wasn't here for us. Dey' wasn't in front uh' our house."

"Where was they at then? You said they was outside…."

"Dey' was across duh' street in front uh' dat' pretty lady's house."

"Oh…I bet they was…she a whore."

Pam and Herby giggled but Baby Girl was not amused. She thought it was a terrible thing to say about her friend but she stayed quiet and listened.

"Why you say dat' mama?" Pam laughed.

"Yeah…why you say dat?" Herby giggled, and received a glare from Pam because she knew only one person could talk to their mother, sparingly, or else she would shut down. She wanted to keep her mother talking and was genuinely interested in the conversation. It was a grownup conversation which she knew she shouldn't be having, and was determined to continue.

"Shut up Herby. Me and mama is talkin!" Pam shouted, and Baby Girl looked on in amazement as she watched Herby frown, and Ellen crack a smile. She forgot her mother always condoned Pam's misbehavior.

Ellen liked that Pam scolded Herby therefore, she continued her conversation, "She a hoe…I know that cause' you ain't never see so many men come outta' a house…. especially if there's no man livin' there…. I may not go outside but I see what's going on. Y'all don't know cause' y'all at school all day but I see um' coming and going all times of the morning. I sit right there in the front winduh' wit' the drapes closed, and I see um."

"What's a whore mama!" Herby burst out, unable to contain his curiosity.

"I told you boy! Don't interrupt when me and mama's talkin!"

"No…it's alright…I guess he's old enough to know."

The children listened closely for they really didn't know what a whore was. They knew it was a bad word that pertained to women but they didn't know the meaning. The word whore, sounded criminal to Baby Girl. She heard children argue while calling each other names they'd say, "That's why yo' mama's a hoe," but they never said whore. She only read that word in literature when describing, a lady of the evening, a woman who took money for sex, a prostitute. Then her mother said the word, removing all doubt.

"Dey's some women out here dat' is some of the nastiest thangs' you could be. Now I know y'all is young but I'd rather you hear this now so you can know what they are, and keep away from them. Dey's called prostitutes. Das' when a woman has sex for money, and you don't wanna' be around nobody das' filthy like dat'. So many men, my lord…. it's disgusting."

"What's sex mama!" Herby was excited now and wanted to know everything.

"Shut up boy! I'll tell ya' when your older!" Pam shouted.

"Oh really....so I guess you know what sex is, huh?" Ellen asked incredulously.

"A little...it's when you touch, and stuff," Pam said shyly.

"Touch and stuff! Naw'.... you don't know what sex is!"

Ellen was upset now because her mind traveled back to the reason why her children's father was unfaithful. It was hookers who destroyed their union. With a jolt her memory engaged, uncovering feelings she had buried, until only anger remained.

"Well, Imma a tell ya', it's nothing pretty or romantic. It's when you put your mouth on some little boys' pee pee! Or let him stick his pee pee in yo' privates," she said pointing her finger between Pam's legs as she sat at the kitchen table.

"Iwwww!" Herby exclaimed, but Pam was too shocked to speak and only held her mouth open in astonishment.

"Das' not right! Dat' can't be right! You didn't say nuthin' bout' kissin' and holdin' hands!" Herby continued.

"Haaa Haa Haa Ha! Is that what you thank!" Ellen laughed outright now and continued to laugh boisterously as she leaned against the stove. It had been some time since her children saw her laugh so they all looked at one another for confirmation.

Baby Girl thought about how she saw men leaving in the night from Cleopatra's house and realized the number of daily visitors was greater than she thought because she didn't know about the ones in the morning. Now she began to think about when she didn't see visitors at night, maybe it was because they came earlier that day.

"Das' right..." Ellen continued laughing as she described sex in more graphic details.

"See boy, when you get older your pee pee's gonna' get hard like dis," she said while pointing her index finger straight. "At first it's gonna' be like dis," she said with her finger limp, "But when you're ready for sex it gets hard," she continued as she pointed her finger straight again, and laughed at the sight of her son looking nervously at his pants.

"Yeah, that's right, it's gonna' get hard, and the girl...this is the girl," she said looking at Pam while making a peace sign with her other hand. "See these two fingers are the girl's legs, see how they open and close," she said while moving her fingers together, then apart, as she giggled. "When the girl's ready for sex she opens her legs like dis'... and the boy sticks his thang' in there, cause' it's hard now," she said, and thrust her index finger in and out of the peace sign, repeatedly, laughing boisterously again, frightening her children.

"Iwwww, stop dat' mama, dat' can't be right, I don't want my thang' gettin' hard, if that's what sex is I don't wanna' do it! You see what mama's doin' Tee Tee? Make her stop!" he yelled, and ran over to Baby Girl. Being five, the act of sexual intercourse was too much information for him to comprehend, so his sister led him from the kitchen and took him upstairs.

It was spring now and the weather was warm so children began to play outside once again. On this particular day Baby Girl was heading to the store to get some things when she ran into Cleopatra.

"Hi my dear, I haven't seen you in a while. How are you?" Cleo said with a smile.

"I'm ok, how are you?"

"I'm well, thanks for asking..." she said, holding out her hand to Baby Girl who grasped it, and the two played mother and daughter while walking to the store, merrily talking about how they spent the winter months. Cleo told her about an island in the West Indies called Jamaica, where the weather was always warm and the people were all shades of color, with some inhabitants from China sprinkled amongst them. Their language was hard to understand even though it was English because their accent was so thick, but she tried her best to imitate it.

"Yes, they say things like.... they don't pronounce certain words...if they say... things, they don't pronounce the, T... H... they just pronounce the, T... so, they say, bring the ting' mon'...go get the ting' mon'...what ting ya' talkin' bout' mon."

Baby Girl laughed as Cleo tried to speak in her best Jamaican accent and made hand motions as she talked.

"Yes....and they say mon'... after everything, and they suck their teeth a lot, and they say tree... instead of three."

"For real?'

"Yeah mon' me want tree Red Snapper mon' yes mon' me say tree." They both laughed.

Cleopatra felt alive when she was with Baby Girl and wanted to keep her. Since she didn't have any children of her own, by choice, she knew she could care for Baby Girl better than her neglectful mother. She would get her infatuation ready for school each morning. They could talk while she cooked breakfast and drank coffee. She needed to interact with that delightfully inquisitive mind, because it was new to the world and desired to absorb everything. Baby Girl's mind energized her, it made her feel like all their conversations were meaningful and every word they exchanged, important. Cleo felt she could settle into a routine of enjoying the morning with her, then entertaining Johns after Baby Girl went to school. She figured she could alter her schedule around her infatuations' life. When school was out in the summer, they could go on vacation together since Cleopatra was lonely. She moved a lot so it was hard to make friends and keep her profession a secret. She only had conversations with one of her clients, the older man that Baby Girl spied most frequently, but their talks were limited. Cleo couldn't wait to retire and take the little princess with her. Her favorite thought was escaping with her precious, and raising the little gem as her own, and maybe even calling her, daughter. This fantasy made her smile in lonely times, and she longed for the winter to end so she could see her jewel again. The thought of having Baby Girl for a daughter gradually seeped into her life, adding joy, purpose, and light to the darkness. She figured she would sacrifice her life now, to live a normal life later. She was grateful not to be poor, so she endured all the dangers in her profession. Having excess money gave Cleopatra freedom, and was the only thing keeping her sane.

  As they approached the store their conversation was abruptly interrupted. Three men were standing near the entrance and one of them called out to Cleo.

  "Hey good lookin'," he said with a smile. He was a scraggly man whose looks had long gone, but his bravado was still intact.

  She tried to ignore him but with his friends' encouragement he boldly continued.

  "I've seen you up there on the hill in the summer time, relaxing."

  "Have you now," she said coldly.

  "Yeah, and I also seen dem' mens comin' outta' yo' house. Whatchu' havin' meetings in there." His friends couldn't contain their amusement and laughed loudly.

  "How I git' in on one uh' dem' meetings? I need ta' come by and see what it's all about."

  "You come anywhere near my house and you'll get hurt!"

"Yeah, I reckon not. I probably ain't got enough money anyway," he stated with a sad expression as he moved closer to the entrance, blocking her path. "I hear dem' boys gotta' pay dues when dey' come ta' visit." He was smiling again, and smacked the hands of his two friends, looking back to her he continued, "And I hear dem' dues is mighty high!" The men laughed heartily as Cleopatra looked down at Baby Girl, still holding her hand she was mortified when their eyes met, but Baby Girl was unaware of the meaning of his cryptic comments. She only understood that he knew about Cleo having male visitors too.

"Come on dear, let's get away from these crazy fools!" she yelled as she pulled Baby Girl passed the man and received a smack on her butt for her efforts. She screamed above the laughter at this disrespectful man.

"Don't you touch me! Don't you dare' put your hands on me. You ain't got no respect treating me like this in front of my daughter. No respect at all!"

Baby Girl couldn't believe her ears. Did she hear Cleopatra correctly? Did she claim her as her daughter? Was she pretending to be her mother? The thought caused her to smile. The vision of them living together, growing old together, eclipsed her mind, blanketing it with joy, but it only lasted a moment.

"I don't know what you talkin' bout'. She ain't no kin to you. That ain't yo' daughter. Das' little bit from up duh' street. She crazy Ellen's daughter. I seen her before. Her an' dem' other pygmies."

"Oh shut up fool! You ever touch me again I'll have somebody break your legs!"

"That may be, but I know Ellen wouldn't like you playin' house wit' her child. She don't like yo' kind, and she wouldn't want you touchin' her. Filth…ain't dat' what she call um' Checkers?" he said, addressing one of the men who got this nickname from his love of the game. The man shook his head in agreement. "Naw' she wouldn't like dat' at all. Maybe I should go over there and tell her what's going on."

"You can tell her whatever you want. You better stay away from me you crazy bastard!" she screamed as she stormed off.

On their way home Cleopatra talked to Baby Girl about her dreams of taking her away, and the importance of investing in real estate, stocks and mutual funds. She spoke quickly as if they were running out of time, as if their escape needed to be soon. She instinctively knew her presence was arousing too much attention, especially if the tramp and his friends at the store knew about her visitors then other people must know too. It was a lot for her infatuation to comprehend, however, Baby Girl did realize that Cleo cared enough to want to raise her, and teach her how to become wealthy. As they approached her home Baby Girl released Cleo's hand and skipped down the walkway to the front door. She noticed the curtains move and realized someone was looking out the front window. She turned and waved to Cleo who was crossing the street, heading home, towards the end of the block. Once inside her house Baby Girl immediately heard her mother yelling.

"Whatchu' doin' wit' dat' hoe! I told you she a prostitute!"

"She's not a prostitute, she's nice!"

"Oh, she nice huh! I saw you holdin' hands wit' her. You know what she do wit' her hands. If you did you'd be washing yours right now. She be holdin' dicks, and playin' wit' dicks, and suckin' um', and kissin' on um', and stickin' um' between her legs, with every man you see go in dat' house, all of um', now that's disgusting!"

"She don't do that mama. She's not like that!"

"How you know? She don't do it for nothing. They give her money ta' do it! That's what a prostitute is, stupid! The men pay her to be nasty! You saw for yourself how many men come ta' see her! It's filthy…she's a dirty hoe!"

Baby Girl was quiet as she thought about what the bum said at the corner store. His riddles began to make sense now. When he joked about paying dues, she understood now. He was talking about the money the men gave Cleo for sex. Her thoughts were interrupted when her mother burst out the front door. Ellen's rage overpowered her. The thought of Baby Girl befriending a prostitute upset her so, it propelled her forward out of her seclusion and into the world, screaming, ready to fight.

She a hoe! She a prostitute! That bitch right dare! That nasty stinkin' bitch right dare' is a hoe!" She yelled and pointed at Cleopatra who was only steps from home. It was an early Saturday morning but there were still a few people outside that looked at Cleo and thought surely Ellen must be mistaken, but two neighbors did shake their head in agreement and frowned at the golden brown, statuesque model, for they too had seen the traffic of men and believed Ellen. Cleopatra saw the attention, and heard the commotion, and turned to see Ellen screaming and pointing at her. Ellen remained on the porch since it was the first time, she came outside in eight months. When she made eye contact with Cleo her anger compelled her to stay, and continue her tirade.

"Yeah, I'm talkin' ta' you, you nasty bitch! You better stay away from my daughter you stinkin' whore! I don't want you nowhere near her, she might catch one uh' dem' diseases you got, you filthy animal! Imma' call the cops on you! We can't have no prostitutes round here, round our kids, spreadin' that filth! She a hoe! Everybody…look at her, right dare, she's a prostitute, she a hoe!" Ellen was frantic now as Baby Girl looked from the curtains and saw Cleo drop her head, and crumple her body from the effect of the truth being revealed, then slowly disappear into her home. Only then did Ellen come inside, however, her tirade continued.

"I don't want you being round that whore no more, you understand me!"

Baby Girl shared Cleo's sadness as she went upstairs while her mother continued to scream, she was greeted by her curious siblings.

"What mama cursing for?"

"She mad cause' I was with Cleopatra."

"Oh, that's nuthin' I thought it was sumthin' serious. You never do nuthin' bad."

Baby Girl ignored Pam and lay on the bed, worried she wouldn't be able to see her friend again. She sat on the porch that afternoon and stared at Cleo's house, hoping to get a glimpse of her while Pam and Herby played. That evening after supper she lay awake spying the house again to no avail. There was no sighting of Cleo and no male visitors. The next day, Sunday, was a cold day so the children stayed indoors as Baby Girl sat near the front window and spied Cleo's house, hoping to see her, but it wasn't to be. That evening, again there were no male visitors, causing her to have a sleepless night from worry. The thought of Cleo's departure saddened her. She couldn't have gone already. It was an unlikely friendship but one they both needed. Unfortunately, Cleopatra couldn't bear being exposed and snuck away in the night, regrettably leaving her precious, along with her happiness. She needed to be refreshed so she took a morning flight to Saint Martin, in the Caribbean, attempting to regain her sanity after being embarrassed, afraid her depression would cause self, destruction, she was determined to control it.

The next day, Monday, was a school day and since Ellen usually stayed in bed during the morning, Baby Girl boldly decided to defy her. She had to see Cleo, she had to know if she was alright so she crossed the street and went to her house, ignoring the protest from Pam. There was no answer when she rang the bell so she knocked, moderately at first, but gradually harder, she banged and kicked the door while calling out Cleopatra's name, unconcerned about the noise or being seen.

"Come on Tee Tee! Ain't nobody there. You gonna' get us in trouble!" Pam called out, but she really wasn't worried. She was more amused than anything. She thought it was funny seeing her sister so frantic to see a prostitute. Finally, she gave up and sadly returned to Pam and they walked to school together.

"You crazy. I don't know why you wanna' be friends with a hoe."

"You shut up!" Baby Girl yelled and pushed Pam to the ground, then continued walking to school in silence, thinking of the friend she lost, thinking about the life they could have had.

XIII

ELLEN GRADUALLY AWAKENS

Ellen awakens as Pam falls in with a destructive crowd. Gradually she emerges from her depression with the help of her Uncle Stanley, who bought her a car because she was afraid to take the bus since it made her nervous to be around people. It was a used car, nothing fancy, but it was sufficient, reliable, and it served its purpose. One day he came to see Baby Girl's report card. She was in the sixth grade now. He was so proud of her because she was a straight "A" student. He asked about Ellen just to be courteous, and was surprised to learn she was bathing, and cooking.

"She ain't stayin' up in her room all day?" he asked.

"No sir."

It was Stanley's custom to sit in his car in front of their house and talk to her. He'd usually have a gift, or a crisp five, dollar bill. He wanted to encourage her excellent class work with a reward. Even though she liked school and was self, motivated, she was happy to have someone besides teachers interested in her studies.

"What's she doing now? Is she feeling alright for company? Is she dressed?"

"Yes, she's dressed. She looks okay. She's wearing clean clothes and her hair is combed. She's a lot better now, before she only wore her dirty robe and slippers."

"Maybe I'll go in and say hello. You think that'll be okay."

"I guess so. She hasn't had company in a while."

Baby Girl led him to the front door, entered the house, then called out for her mother.

"Mama.... uncle Stanley's here!"

She figured her mother might be in the kitchen but Herby and Pam came running down the stairs, answering her call instead. They were always happy to see their uncle because he was friendly and gave them money.

"Uncle Stanley! Uncle Stanley! Uncle Stanley!" they

screamed in unison as they ran into his outstretched arms.

"How's my favorite crumb snatchers? Y'all been good?" he asked as he rummaged through his pockets.

"We been good!" they exclaimed excitedly.

"Well since you been good let's see what I have for you," he replied and gave them each a dollar.

"Thank you, Uncle Stanley!" they shouted and ran back upstairs passing their mother on her way down.

"Stanley is that you? It's been so long.... Sorry I look a mess. I wish I would've known you was comin' in, I would've straightened the place up. These kids runnin' round' leavin' a trail uh' dirt. Y'all come back down here and cleanup yuh' mess!"

It was Saturday morning and Ellen wore her hair in two pony tails. Her navy blue, bell bottom, jeans and yellow cotton shirt, with a wide lapel that was tied at the waist, were neat and clean. Stanley was pleased with her appearance. Wearing her hair in this fashion made her resemble the little girl he remembered. He was relieved to see the confusion in her eyes had gone, replaced with clarity, assuring him that she was getting better.

"I got some bacon, eggs and grits on the stove, you hungry?"

"Nah' I ate earlier but I will have some coffee if you have any."

Even though the food enticed him with its delicious aroma, he didn't want to take any away from the kids, knowing the family was on hard times.

The catalyst for Ellen's waning depression was the occurrence of two things. First, when her despair was severe, she glimpsed at her reflection in the mirror by chance, because she avoided mirrors and turned them facing the wall. This particular mirror hung on the inside of her closet door, which was left open. She glanced at her likeness, wondering who this stranger was since her appearance had changed. She had always been chubby but since misery took away her appetite, she only digested crushed ice, causing her to lose weight. She stood in front of the mirror, captivated, staring into her reflection, slowly disrobing, dropping her house coat to the floor around her feet like a butterfly emerging from its cocoon, gradually getting accustomed to her image. She raised her hands above her head and turned to see every angle of her body. Seeing her ribs surprised her so she felt them, slowly running her fingers over them in disbelief since she was never able to do this before, because they were covered with fat. She was pleased and stood back to view her new self with clarity.

The second occurrence that caused Ellen's depression to subside was a letter she received from her beloved, the children's father, Baby Fats. She was unaware that he was trying to contact her because she didn't have a telephone. He was in prison and mailed her a letter from jail. He was remorseful. Being incarcerated, and sober, caused him to regret treating her badly, as a result he expressed his feelings in a two, page letter. Even though they weren't together she still loved him and wanted him back. She cherished the letter because it was years since her beloved expressed desire for her. She used the letter as her strength and read it daily. The tender words empowered her. They made her smile and caused her heart to beat joyfully. Her personality returned in increments, while her appearance sharpened because she was subconsciously preparing herself for his return.

Pam was nine and gradually became estranged from Baby Girl, who was excelling in school while she was a truant. She felt neglected since her sister stopped trying to force her to go to school, and mistakenly thought she no longer loved her, but this wasn't true. Baby Girl did love her however, she had an old soul and was unremorseful when Pam decided to ignore her guidance. She remembered all the unsuccessful times she tried to keep her from stealing. She recalled the multiple requests she made for her to attend school, even offering to tutor her, to no avail. She was frustrated and decided to pursue her own happiness and leave Pam alone to do whatever she wanted. She figured since their mother was getting better, she would have to discipline her.

On one occasion, when Pam was playing hooky from school, she ran into some twelve, year old kids, who lived two blocks away. It was early in the afternoon when the bad kids were hanging out at the corner store, playing the pin ball games located in the back. It grew congested so the owner only let kids inside who had money. It was too crowded for bystanders, "Only paying customers," he would say. She stood and watched as three boys gathered around one of the games. They looked suspicious because they weren't playing it. The first boy was tall, heavyset, caramel complexioned and frowning with his arms folded. It was his intent to be intimidating because he was the enforcer, the muscle, the one who held their victims while the other two searched their pockets. The next boy was coffee tinted and smaller, with an average size and build. He wished he was as tough as his friend but since he wasn't, he took the role as the backup, the lookout, the one who barked but didn't bite, the one who threatened kids to weed out the scared ones. The third boy was onyx. He was short, shorter than Pam, and wore oversized clothes. He was the smartest amongst them, the brains of the crew. He was the one who planned their crimes, and they followed him because his schemes where successful.

  They stood with their backs to the game, and when other children attempted to play it, they would glare at them menacingly, and frighten them away. That's what drew her attention initially. She was always attracted to bullies because she was one. She enjoyed taking advantage of kids, making them do her bidding, making weaker, sensitive children cry, but she never took money from them by force, strong armed them, or extorted them. These kids were robbers and to her delight they were about to show their skills right in front of her.

  She noticed as the brain took out a big brown paper bag and knelt down next to the area where coins are inserted in the pin ball machine. He pulled a long screw driver from inside his coat and used it to pry open the cash box, as his two friends concealed him with their bodies while looking out for the owner, who walked around periodically surveying the area. After a few tries he pried enough of the metal loose to get to the coins. The noise was muffled by the atmosphere in the game room as the quarters dropped into the bag. The brain wore a navy blue, oversized coat called a Snorkel, because of the shape of its hood. When the hood is zipped closed it curved into a funnel, protruding forward like the end of a telescope, giving the wearer tunnel vision, concealing the sides of the face but also protecting from inclement weather. The hood had imitation fur surrounding the edges that resembled a graying German shepherd, while the material of the coat was a water proof nylon, polyester mix. When the brain pulled the hood over his head all Pam could see were the whites of his eyes and teeth, when he smiled, once he noticed her watching. He put his finger to his lips in a shushing sign, then motioned her with his chin to keep watch for the owner, mouthing the words, look out. She was glad to help, and walked around looking for the owner but he was nowhere to be found. He was in the front of the store assisting his two workers; a middle aged, overweight, auburn complexioned woman at the cash register, and a lanky, chocolate toned, stock boy, who was a great help and enabled the owner to be in two places at once.

    The stock boy truly ran the store, having worked there for three years, starting when he was seventeen. He knew where everything was located, refilled merchandise, ordered supplies, worked the register when the cashier was on lunch, and ran errands to the bank for the owner. Since he was young, the owner relied on his strength and quickness because sometimes he would have to chase kids away or break up fights. He was the first to see the trio leaving the game room, coming towards the front of the store followed by a scraggly, chubby girl. He was familiar with them, having seen the boys in the neighborhood. They only came into the store occasionally and always caused trouble. They usually started a commotion or harassed other kids, and he knew to watch them. They surprised him today because he didn't see them arrive, if he had, he would have kept an eye on them, but he was busy helping customers and stocking the shelves when they entered.

    As they approached the front, he noticed the short, onyx boy, wearing the oversized coat, seemed to be holding something underneath it, as he walked with his arms folded around his stomach, securing whatever he was carrying. The stock boy, Luther, suspected he was stealing so he rushed from behind the counter to confront the group. The enforcer blocked him from grabbing the brain, and Pam marveled at the scuffle that ensued as it quickly turned to chaos. She saw the surprise in Luther's eyes when he felt the strength of the younger boy. She smiled devilishly as he struggled to get pass the enforcer but could not. She watched as the brain jumped back, out of reach from his outstretched arms each time Luther tried to grab him. The boys wrestled from side to side in the narrow isle, knocking merchandise from the shelves as they tussled. The lookout joined the fray, believing he and the enforcer could overpower the stock boy, while the children yelled with excitement at the unexpected fracas. Now was the opportunity for the brain to getaway since his cohorts subdued their pursuer, he quickly slipped past them and scampered out the door. Once safe, his partners let the stock boy go and followed the brain. Their victim was embarrassed and angry because they came into the store, disrespecting the place, knowing he worked there. Luther took it personally and stormed after them, enraged. That's when Pam stuck out her foot and tripped him into the gumball machine. When it crashed to the floor, the noise startled the brain and he turned to see the stock boy sprawled out amongst the glass and candy. He saw as Luther angrily grabbed Pam by the hem of her pants, and laughed when she kicked free, then ran to join them. He liked her immediately.

The owner, a short, fat, balding senior citizen, was busy in his small office behind the counter, deeper in the alcove, inspecting his bank statements when he heard the uproar. First, he was startled by the screams of his cashier, followed by the sound of breaking glass. He knew instantly it was the gumball machine sitting by the entrance. He hurried from his office as soon as he heard scuffling sounds and animated children voices.

"Damn kids! Don't y'all be breakin' up my stuff!" he shouted as he burst to the counter and saw children crawling about the floor, unconcerned about their safety as they sifted through pieces of broken glass, clamoring for the brightly colored, marble shaped gumballs, that spilled everywhere.

"Luther! Where you at boy! These damn kids is tearin' up my store! Y'all git' from round' dat' candy fo' yuh' cut yo' self!" he yelled, unsuccessfully, as he waved, and hovered his arms above the youngsters like a magician. The cashier was useless because she was easily stressed. She stayed behind the register nervously stamping her feet as if the children were mice, and flailed her hands around her head while screeching in a high pitch.

This was Pam's initiation into the group and soon she began living at their house, where the children were taught how to shoplift from their mother, and how to rob people from their father. Actually, he was only the father of two of the four children. The mother was short and pretty, with a button shaped nose that resembled a doe. Her body was shapely and she used her looks to help her steal. Her beauty distracted people, seducing them until they were unguarded. Her most lucrative scheme was conning elderly men out of their savings. She cruelly left one of her victim's Bankrupt, causing him to lose his house and move into a retirement facility. The father was short with an onyx complexion similar to his son, the brain. He had a muscular build and a scar across his left cheek from being attacked during his many visits to prison, beginning at age eleven, when he was sent to juvenile detention for stabbing his foster mother in the chest with an ice pick. He didn't tell anyone he stabbed her because she was sexually abusing him, making him touch her before feeding him, starving him unless he caressed her, with the acts becoming increasingly longer and occurring more often, until the day she appeared in the kitchen wearing a long t-shirt with no panties. She sat in a chair and grabbed him by the neck, forcing his face down between her legs; that's how the ice pick incident came about. He tried to free himself from her clutches but he couldn't, because he was a boy and she was a heavyset, strong, woman. In desperation he reached for the ice pick laying on the table and thrust it into her. Only then did she release him, screaming in agony as the blood spilled from her wound. He was deemed a menace by the court and incarcerated in juvenile detention until he turned eighteen. Since there were no guns in jail, he learned the art of robbing individuals by force, strong arming them. Juvenile detention was a training ground for criminals. They were given the opportunity to take classes and earn a high school diploma, but many of the inmates were too violent to attend and would constantly have their class privileges revoked.

    Ellen noticed Pam's absence slowly, over time she began to miss her second born and wondered where she was, so much so that she asked her eldest child her whereabouts, only to learn they were unknown. She was worried because her first born seemed unconcerned. Ellen was distressed because she was used to Baby Girl caring about her sibling's safety, out of necessity, since prior to now, depression had rendered her emotionless. Ellen was not accustomed to saving anyone, but her maternal instincts gingerly returned and clawed at her heart. Moderately, she was unable to sleep, increasingly, her restless nights were caused by nightmares concerning Pam being abducted, tortured, and held against her will. Finally, it bothered her immensely, and propelled her out of the house on this spring morning, compelling her to search for Pam, starting right after her children departed for school. She decided to survey the neighborhood, thinking this would be a good time to find her daughter amongst the other children, but it wasn't meant to be as she drove around, methodically cruising through each block.

    After several unsuccessful attempts, Ellen changed her plan, deciding to search after school, assuming correctly that Pam wasn't going to class so why would she wake up early, no.... she would sleep late, and come out in the afternoon. On this day she parked at the corner of the block where the school was located because she wanted to see the route the children walked. They seemed to break off in separate directions but eventually she discovered three gathering places. A park in the north, a store in the south, and a basketball court on the west side of town. Ellen decided to start with the location closest to the house, a small corner store where children gathered. She learned the store had pinball games inside and that was the main reason so many kids went there. She never saw Pam frequenting the store but made it a point to drive by regularly in hopes of a chance encounter.

    The house was empty and quiet. Her children were older now and regularly left unannounced, wandering about unsupervised, coming and going whenever they wanted but usually returning no later than dusk, that is until Pam stopped coming home entirely. She occasionally stayed out overnight so she wasn't missed at first, and the family never sat together at the kitchen table for dinner, therefore, her absence wasn't noticed initially. It was a month into her disappearance when Ellen ventured outside on a wintry Sunday afternoon, which was rare because she hadn't left the house on a Sunday in two years. On this day she was remorseful for being a neglectful mother. She didn't realize how long Pam was missing because her sense of time was gone. Her memory was foggy at first but gradually cleared as her depression subsided. Today, clarity ruled and she couldn't face the reality of Pam's disappearance. The certainty of being an abusive parent worried her. Not knowing if her second born was dead or alive frightened her, motivating her to search for Pam once again.

    Pam knew her mother didn't come outside on Sundays so she was close to the house, at the corner of their street on Wexford Place, casually conversing with her new friends, unaware that her mother was lurking in the shadows, amazed at the sighting of her second born. Ellen was frozen in place, from shock mostly. She was astonished by the sudden vision after walking slowly, methodically wandering, aimlessly drawn to this destination. She felt as though it was fate, being that it was unusual for her to be outside on the Lords, day.

    She didn't want to frighten Pam so she decided to follow her in hopes of discovering where she was staying. She watched as Pam walked away, and waited for a moment before going after her.

It wasn't long before the group of kids reached their destination, a two story, wine-red, brick house, that sat on a hill with two rows of steep, vertical steps leading to the front door. The first five steps were cement, with a four, foot wall accompanying them. The wall contained a mixture of dark, and light gray stones. It surrounded the hill and traveled along in front of the next couple of houses, finally ending at a garage. After the cement steps was a long row of fifteen wooden steps guarded by wooden hand rails, leading to another set of four wooden steps that connected to the porch. Ellen watched as the children ascended the steps and gathered on the small porch that was designed to hold four people comfortably. She stood behind a tree across the street from the house, but felt she'd be discovered now that the children were elevated and could see farther.

    Ellen decided to go home after she discovered Pam's location. Her heart was calm and emotions no longer controlled her. The need to plan her next move caused her mind to engage, transforming anxiety into analytical thought. Her brain guided her actions as she studied the situation. She decided if Pam wasn't home in twenty, four hours, to return to the house, which was her first mistake. She should have known that a day wouldn't make a difference because it was obvious that Pam wasn't coming home voluntarily. When Ellen discovered the house and saw Pam going inside, she should have confronted her. The shock of seeing her daughter unharmed and cheerful turned her sadness into rage. How dare her second born cause her to worry.

    Monday came and went with no appearance from Pam, therefore, by Tuesday Ellen decided to visit the house on the hill in hopes of seeing her daughter again. This time she drove and parked close by. She sat in the car for thirty minutes, watching the house, seeing a mixture of teenager's present, intimidated her. They were so animated and active as they ran on the hill, tussling with one another, full of energy as they played on the stairs. She didn't know if she could confront Pam under these circumstances. Feeling her nerves weaken she drove away, never exiting the car, heading in the direction of the small corner store when she saw Pam walking behind three boys. She was busy fumbling with a stolen bag of potato chips when Ellen surprised her by screeching to a halt and shouting from the car window, which was her second mistake. If Ellen had been calm and friendly, she would have made her daughter feel at ease, and receptive to conversation. Ellen was unaware of her inability to control her anger, so to her detriment, rage caused her to act negatively.

"Pam! Pam! Git' yo' ass over here! Where the hell you been? Got me worryin' sick about you while you out here runnin' the streets!"

Pam was startled and dropped the chips as she jumped back from the curb. Naturally her friends were curious and inquired about the crazy lady.

"You alright lil' bit! Why dat' lady screamin' at chu' like dat?"

"Das' my momma. I thought she was sick but I guess she feelin' better."

"Yo' momma, word...das' messed up...."

"Pam! Pam, you hear me talkin' ta' you!" Ellen was frantic as she beeped the horn to accompany her screams, drawing attention from bystanders, curious as to why she was accosting this girl until she revealed her identity.

"Das' my daughter! Das' my daughter right dare'! She a runaway! She ain't supposed ta' be out here! She dun' ran away from home! She a runaway!"

Ellen shouted and pointed at Pam, making her nervous because she knew that a runaway was a bad thing, but never considered herself to be one. Pam wasn't homeless and thought all runaways were. She had a home but just wasn't going there, not because she was abused or that it was a bad environment, but because it was boring. Her mother ignored her, not that she cared, and her siblings were busy with their friends and had their own lives. They weren't close like they were growing up since Baby Girl no longer took care of them. She was the one who kept them together and raised them during the troubled years when their mother couldn't, but now everything was different.

Even though she was free from the clutches of depression, Ellen wasn't nurturing her children. She didn't know how to teach them constructively. Now that her mind was clear, her main function was cooking and cleaning. She was vigilant in being neat and hygienic. She made sure her children were bathed and fed, the two youngest mostly since Baby Girl was self-sufficient, and Pam was absent. Now paranoia replaced depression. Ellen was afraid of the outside world. She was a pessimist and unknowingly stressed her children with her worrying, telling them to be careful of everything, no matter how great or small, nothing was considered safe.

Ellen jumped from the car to apprehend her daughter but Pam was too quick and ran off. Her friends just watched as Ellen chased behind her unsuccessfully, as Pam zigzagged from side to side, avoiding Ellen's outstretched arms, causing her to stumble and trip as Pam ducked and dodged her clutches, as the boys to roared with laughter. Then Ellen returned to confront them, which was her third mistake. They weren't afraid of some crazy lady even if it was Pam's mother, but this did keep them from physically attacking her out of respect for their friend, however, it didn't keep them from verbally attacking her.

"I seen y'all before! Y'all ain't nuthin' but some no, good, ghetto rats! What y'all doin' wit' my daughter! She only nine! Y'all ain't supposed ta' be hangin' out wit' little girls!"

The trio laughed at her inaccuracy. The thought of them following anyone was absurd.

"You crazy lady. We ain't hangin' out wit' her, she following us around, keep tellin' us she ain't got nowhere ta' go, keep tellin' us she hungry and need a place ta' stay. So, we felt sorry for the little runt and took her in," the brain explained even though he didn't have to.

"She lyin' then, cause' I'm her mama and she got a home! She got food and clothes and don't need no one ta' take care of her!"

"Yeah she do…you said so yourself, she only nine. She not supposed to be wandering around alone, but she is."

"She ain't alone! She got a family! It's my job ta' raise her, not yours!"

"You're doing a terrible job…" the boys laughed at the truth being told. "Anyway, we ain't tryin' ta' raise her, just saving her from yo' crazy ass…." The laughter continued and caused her anger to erupt into action as she moved closer to the trio. She raised her hands with her fingers spread wide as though she was going to snatch one of them. The enforcer frowned, balled his hands into fists and stared menacingly at Ellen. She was accustomed to children running when confronted by adults, but these were pre-teens, they were tough, and weren't about to retreat, in fact, the enforcer had to be stopped from hitting her. The brain placed his hand on the enforcer's chest, signaling him not to attack, but he knew if Ellen continued to approach, he wouldn't be able to stop his friend from beating her.

"Whatchu' gonna' do! You gonna' hit a woman!"

"Sho' will….and you ain't no woman…just some crazy lady. You lucky we know your daughter or else you woulda' already been beat up. Now git' on outta' here fo' I change my mind!"

The boys humor returned as Ellen backed away, retreated to her car, and threatened them before leaving.

"Dis' ain't over! I know where you live! You tell Pam I'm comin' for her!" she yelled as she sped off.

XIV

PAM RETURNS HOME

Ellen was unemployed. She had nothing to occupy her time. She couldn't call anyone since the telephone was out of service. She didn't have many friends so when the phone did work, she only called her mother, occasionally. She almost never received calls, therefore, when the phone rang it was like an alarm sounding off, startling everyone in the house. The phone was located on the first floor in the kitchen and the children usually answered it, if they were home, to Ellen's displeasure. All she did was cook, clean and watch television, the news mostly, fixating on the crime and turmoil that was happening in her city, and across the country. Because she didn't go outside much, her view of the world was biased and inaccurate. Believing there was no good in society since the news mostly showed people behaving badly, fed her paranoia and caused Ellen to transfer it to her children with actions, and conversations. It usually started like this,

"Y'all better watch out for.... Y'all better be careful cause.... You better not go down their cause.... The news said stay away from that area." She never greeted her children with a smile. There was only the look of worry on her face when they saw her after school.

Herby was seven and Candace was five so Ellen drove them to and from school, which was a positive transformation from years prior when she neglectfully let her two oldest children, who were the same ages at the time, venture out alone. She was over protective now, when before she was unconcerned. Herby remembered when Baby Girl took the role as head of household and preferred that arrangement. He could tell his mother didn't quite know what she was doing but appreciated the effort. It was better than her being a zombie. Even though he missed his independence, and having no parental guidance had its benefits, he was happy to have his meals prepared regularly now, when before they were sporadic. He also noticed her driving a different route home. Unknown to him, his mother drove past the house she saw Pam enter, because she assumed that's where Pam was staying. Ellen knew on Monday Baby Girl came home directly after school, therefore, she planned to leave the children in her care, and visit the house.

"Tina... I gotta' go out. I won't be long. Your brotha' and sista' are in the kitchen eating. I told um' ta' be good and not bother you cause' I know you like ta' get your homework done right away. Is that ok?"

"Yes mama. It's okay. They'll be fine."

Ellen was concerned that Baby Girl never asked about Pam. Maybe she knew all along where she was staying.

As usual, there were some kids outside when she arrived at the house. While ascending the steps, Pam appeared and sat on the porch to Ellen's surprise, but upon seeing her mother she was startled and retreated. She couldn't believe her mother was there. 'How did she know where to find me?' She thought, and figured someone told but couldn't understand who. She couldn't comprehend how her mother was functioning, when before she was debilitated. She was selfish and liked when her mother was ill and let her roam freely to do whatever she wanted. Why did she have to be well now when she was having so much fun.

"I saw you! You come out here right now! You betta' git' yo' ass home! You can't be stayin' here wit' deez' people," she screamed when she reached the porch, causing the children on the hill to look.

"Who she talkin' bout?" One of them commented.

"I think she's here for the new girl. The nappy headed chubby one."

Ellen rung the bell. The screen door was locked but the wooden door was open and she could see inside. It was an open area with the staircase six feet away to the right, directly behind the door, leading to the second floor, accompanied by a thick wooden banister anchored by a post, covered with coats. To the left side of the stairway was a smaller, thinner door, located at the end of a short walkway, twenty feet away. Ellen banged on the door when no one answered the bell, and continued yelling until someone finally came. It was the mother who appeared from an archway to the far left, that faced the staircase. The house was designed in such a way that everything was to the left side of the front door since the stairway occupied the right. It was a three, floor home with the attic being large enough to live in since the ceilings were high. The mother looked annoyed and greeted Ellen with an attitude.

"What chu' bangin' on my door like that fo!"

"You got my chil' in dare!"

"I don't know what chu' talkin' bout."

"What! I saw her! Just now, she ran up in here!"

"No, ain't no kids in here, dey' all outside, you sure she's not one uh' dem," she was being coy, but Ellen wasn't amused. In her recovering state, she didn't like when someone questioned her sanity, or played with her mind, it was insulting, and the mother meant for it to be. She was informed of Ellen's condition and believed Pam to be truthful when describing her mother's inability to function. Initially, she would not have let Pam stay if she didn't believe there was neglect, but now that she saw a woman who was functioning and rational, she still hid Pam because she was a good thief.

One of the rules of the house was, if you stayed you had to contribute, and because Pam didn't have any money, she was incorporated into the family business of pilfering. The father guided the older boys and showed them how to rob people while the mother instructed everyone else on the finer points of shoplifting. Pam loved it, and was a quick learner since she was already taking little things whenever she had the opportunity. The mother saw potential in her and taught her how to steal larger items. She didn't have to teach her how to lie and be deceitful since Pam was already an expert at that. She gave her oversized clothes with compartments sewn into them that were specifically for stealing, and was never disappointed when Pam returned with various items the mother requested. She liked that Pam was nine, because even if she was caught the store would let her go, telling her never to come back, after retrieving their property of course, declining to arrest her. No, she wasn't about to give her up willingly, and since Pam didn't want to go, this made her concealment easier.

"You must think I'm a fool if you think I'm lettin' you keep her! She don't need ta' be round' this riff raff. Bunch uh' hoodlums that's what dey' is!"

"Who you callin' a hoodlum?!" One of the teenagers overheard Ellen and was upset at being disrespected by this stranger.

"Keep talkin' lady I'll punch you in the mouth!" the girl retorted to Ellen's surprise, because in the mist of her ranting she was oblivious to the others around her. Suddenly the curtains in the large front window that overlooked the hill, moved, and a small pear, shaped head peaked out from the darkness. Even though the face couldn't be seen Ellen knew immediately it was Pam. Her daughter wanted to observe the confrontation, being unsatisfied listening. She wanted to know how far her mother would go, considering she saw her. This would truly reveal if her mother's mind was healing. In the past Ellen would shut down if things got too stressful, resorting to mumble and loose eye contact. Pam needed to see her mother's reaction so she could determine her next move. She knew if her mother relapsed, she would feel bad since she caused the entire situation, and be compelled to leave with her. On the other hand, if her mother put up a good fight and didn't back down, then she wouldn't feel bad staying because she knew her mother could absorb the rejection.

"Pam, I know das' you in duh' winduh. I see you, ya' little devil. Imma' git' Stanley and we gonna' come back cause' ain't no chil' of mine gonna' be runnin' round' wit' some thieves!" she yelled and stormed off. Of course, she didn't know for a fact that they were thieves, but she figured anyone associated with her daughter, and letting her stay at their house had to be crooked.

Once Ellen drove off the mother confronted Pam.

"I thought you said she was sick and didn't leave the house."

"She was. I guess she's better now."

"Oh, you think so," the mother replied sarcastically. "Listen here little girl. You don't lie to me. I don't care what chu' say and do in dem' streets but when you come in my house you act right. You understand me?"

"Yes mam...."

The brain appeared at the top of the stairs and called out to Pam. He was on the second floor the whole time and heard the conversation.

"Hey lil' bit, come here, I wanna' talk to you!"

He was planning his next caper and could use her help. When Pam reached the second floor, she met his pals in the first room to the left. There were three rooms and a bathroom on the second floor, the smallest being the one they were in, the largest being the one next to the bathroom, the parent's room, which faced a smaller, narrower set of stairs that led to the third floor where the rest of the children stayed.

"I wanna' show you something," he said, and led her into the room where the enforcer and the lookout were huddled over a table as if they were studying for a test. There was a chess game on the table but the board was turned over so no boxes where shown. Only a few pieces sat on the board in various positions; a King, Rook, Knight, Queen and Bishop. It was the first time Pam saw chess pieces outside of a picture, or magazine. She saw checkers before but they were flat and ordinary. She liked the chess pieces and if she weren't among friends, she would've taken one, the King.

"I have an idea how we can rob the Woolworth store downtown."

It was his most daring caper yet. He was tired of nickel and dime, two, bit jobs, and wanted a bigger payday. He thought it was an original scheme but it wasn't. Not understanding the scope of life, disregarding those who lived thousands of years before him, he naively believed his plan was new, but no matter, it was a good idea. It was called a smash and grab. That's when you get a group of people together and by sheer number, and the advantage of surprise, you smash a window or display case, grab as many items as you can, then run out of the store. The brain planned to use a crowbar to smash the jewelry display case in the store. He specifically wanted wrist watches. He already had customers to sell them to, and if they weren't interested there was always the pawn shop. Yes, it was a good plan, it had its risk but he believed with proper preparation they would be successful. That's why Pam was brought into the scheme. He needed more people, the trio was solid, five would be ideal but he would have to settle with four. He liked the fact that she was a little girl and would use this to their advantage.

"Sit over here. I wanna' show you what we're planning," he motioned to Pam and she joined the other two at the table. The enforcer and the lookout argued over the same chess piece, the King.

"You betta' let it go if you know what's good for you!" the enforcer barked, bringing the matter to a close by making a fist. The lookout would argue all day but when it came to violence, he wanted no part of it since he knew his adversary was much stronger. The brain began explaining the plan.

"This is me," he said taking the Rook and positioning it on

the board. He liked this piece because it was shaped like a castle.

"Willie this is you," he addressed the enforcer, showing him where to place his piece. The lookout chose the Knight as his piece because it was shaped like the head of a horse. Pam was given the Queen as her piece to her delight. Now the brain continued explaining as he moved the pieces about, showing each person what their actions should be, where the jewelry case was located and when they would strike. The enforcer was given the responsibility of breaking the glass display because he was the strongest, the brains would collect the watches, the lookout and Pam were the decoys, they would create a diversion.

There were two exits each protected by a security guard. They planned to commit their crime a half an hour before closing. It was the easiest time to enter the store with the least suspicion. It would be difficult since they were unaccompanied minors, which was a giveaway, a tip off that criminal activity was eminent. They would be profiled as shoplifters, especially if they entered together, so the brain and the enforcer would enter from the front and the lookout and Pam would enter from the rear, separately of course. Getting downtown was another obstacle. Deciding to take the bus and in need of cash, the group passed a hotdog cart. The brain saw the tip jar sitting next to the bread rolls and realized that was the answer to their money problem.

The hotdog vendor was in his forties, short in stature, fat, and wore an apron and a coin belt for his quarters, nickels and dimes. Sure, the brain knew he could run off with the jar but that would cause too much commotion. He didn't want the vendor chasing them, even though he was sure they wouldn't be caught, or yelling to alert others. He knew a quiet, discrete pilfering was needed, if such a thing were possible. He decided to use Pam since she appeared innocent and vulnerable. He planned to use the same tactic at Woolworths, having already discussed it with Pam, he knew she was familiar with the routine.

"Hey lil' bit, you see the hotdog man. He's got a tip jar on his cart, and we need the money for the bus fare to get downtown."

She immediately smiled. She loved stealing and was happy to help.

"What chu' want me ta' do!"

"Just go over there and tell him you're lost and need directions. It's the same thing you're gonna' say to the guard at the store so do like we practiced, but stand behind him, make him turn around, give him the sad face, you know, keep his attention while I take the money out the jar. Think you can do that?"

"No problem, I can do it."

"And you two look out. Keep watch for people trying to buy something. Give me time to get the money."

"We got chu."

Pam approached the vendor as the trio stood nearby waiting for the moment, she got his attention. When he turned his back to address her, the brain made his move, trying to be invisible as he slid up to the cart while his friends stood watch.

"Mr…… Do you know where Chambersburg Road is? I'm lost," Pam whimpered in her best baby voice, looking as sad as possible.

"I sure do. It's a longways off though. What you doin' out here by yourself? Where your parents at?"

He was completely engrossed in their conversation, unsuspecting, not knowing the brain was at his cart crouching to make himself even smaller as he quietly snatched the tip jar and stuck it inside his oversized coat, then quickly walked off. It was a smooth crime with only one witness. A middle-aged lady saw the theft and was surprised at the boldness of it. She never saw someone commit a crime, and being an upstanding citizen with morals and values, she was about to alert the vendor when the enforcer intervened, blocking her path as she approached.

"Where you goin' lady!" he scowled, and scared her off. She was nervous to begin with so when he approached her, she instinctively smiled, since she greeted everyone this way, but to be met with a menacing scowl in return, as if she had done something insolent towards him, alarmed her, and made her momentarily forget informing. I say momentarily because when Pam saw the boys leaving, she abruptly followed them, thanking the vendor before he was finished talking, giving the woman another chance to approach, unhindered this time. When she reached the vendor, he was looking about the grass thinking the tip jar must have fallen.

"Sir, sir they took your jar," she informed.

"Who took my jar?"

"Those kids right there," she pointed and the vendor had to squint and focus his eyes because the thieves were some distance away. He could barely make them out but did recognize the turquoise pants Pam wore, and realized she was part of the theft since she walked along with the group. Her deception hurt him, particularly since he thought she was lost and tried to help her, only to find out that it was all a lie, a distraction to get his attention away from the money. He was upset now and screamed after them, flailing his arms while announcing he was robbed and pointing in their direction.

"They robbed me! Those kids over there! They stole my tip jar! Stop… thief! Stop… thief! Somebody, get a cop! The police are never around when you need them." He turned to the lady and thanked her, knowing that it was a slim chance catching the culprits. At least he was aware of the scheme and would be careful the next time someone came to distract him. He would tie the jar to the cart from now on so it couldn't be removed so easily. He had to have a tip jar, that's how he made extra money. He knew times were changing for the worst since in the old days, no one would have attempted such a blatant theft in the daylight.

The kids were unaware that their crime was discovered and didn't hear the vendors screams.

"We better get rid of this jar," the brain said as he pulled it from his coat. It was the size of a thirty, two once pickle jar and the children were happy to see a few dollar bills mixed in amongst the coins. They divided the money, each getting about three dollars and fifty cents, and waited for the bus that traveled to the city. Fortunately for them the bus arrived quickly, in minutes, because the vendor and the woman had the attention of a few people, and called the police.

The bus ride was uneventful as they rode downtown. They sat in the back and went over the plan again. Pam would enter the store last from the rear. It was her job to get the guards attention by claiming she was lost, so he would leave his post to help her. The rear entrance was also the escape route and the element of surprise was their ally.

It was twenty minutes after seven when they arrived at the store on a Wednesday evening. The day and time they planned. The brain figured less people would be there since the store was closing at eight o'clock. Once inside they would wait until seven forty, five to strike. This would give Pam time to accomplish her part of the plan. The brain knew they announced lost children over the PA system, which would be their signal to attack. Just in case the announcement occurred before the allotted time, he figured they should get in position. He met the enforcer on the second floor, they made eye contact, standing apart at first, inconspicuous, not wanting to draw attention. He stood on one side of the floor and the enforcer stood on the other. The lookout was in the children department on the second floor too, in the rear, waiting for the signal, waiting to emerge and distract the cashier at the jewelry counter while his buddies smashed the display glass and snatched the watches. He acted as if he were shopping, as instructed. He was not supposed to stand like a statue, and wait, it would make him look suspicious. The brain already knew how to blend in with the shoppers, even though they were sparse, he browsed the aisles in the kitchen section, picking up various items pretending to inspect them.

"Attention shoppers we have a lost child," the announcement blared over the speakers. "A nine, year old girl wearing greenish blue pants, black shoes and a black coat, is lost," there was a pause, then inaudible, soft chatter, then the announcement continued, "Her name is Gretchen…. she can be found at the security office located in the basement."

The brain quickly walked to the jewelry counter and knelt down, pretending to tie his shoe laces, waiting for the enforcer while unzipping the top of his coat, revealing the curved part of the crow bar. The jewelry counter was shaped like a rectangle with an island in the middle that restricted the view from one side to the other, which worked in their favor since the lookout was to stand on the opposite side where the female pieces were located, and keep the sales lady busy by lying about wanting to buy a present for his mother. What he would say was rehearsed.

The enforcer quickly emerged from his position and stood over his partner at the counter. He was already wearing black, leather, gloves, when he reached into brains coat to retrieve the crow bar. Then the brain put on his gloves as his partner took a baseball hitters stance, swinging as hard as he could, hitting the glass display case with a thunderous boom, alerting everyone on the second floor. The sound surprised them. It was the only thing the brain hadn't anticipated. The sales lady jumped, frightened, knowing immediately it was her counter display glass. She ignored the lookout as he tried to keep her attention. He reached out to grab her by the arm but was hindered by the width of the counter. She peaked around the island just in time to see the enforcer strike the glass again, since it didn't break but only cracked on the first swing. This time the glass shattered, falling to the floor in little pieces and falling inside amongst the watches too. The brain pulled out a duffle bag as the sales lady screamed, then ran from behind the counter. He knew she was going to tell security, knowing they only had moments to spare he reached in and grabbed as many watches as he could, shoving them into the bag, four, five, six, seven, he mentally counted, filling the bag to capacity, cutting his right wrist on one of the sharp, pointed, glass spikes, since he never cleared them from the edges of the counter before reaching in. After the initial surprise some customers drew near out of curiosity, wondering what caused the explosion, viewing the conclusion of the robbery.

"Hey man, people is comin!" the lookout yelled.

"Well, keep em' away, we almost done!"

One shopper in particular, an older man, tried to interfere.

"You boys stop that right now!" he screamed as he approached the counter, coming closer as other shoppers stayed away, only observing. This man wasn't afraid of preteens and was determined to do something. The lookout ran from his side of the counter and stood between the man and his partners. He knew the man was too big for him to physically impede so he had to scare him, but how, he wondered. Suddenly he remembered the old time, gangster movies he loved to watch, and knew what to do, but he wasn't sure it would work. He zipped his coat halfway down and shoved his hand inside, under his chest near his waist band, and scowled, "You take another step and I'll blow your head off." He bluffed the man by faking he carried a gun, and it worked, stopping the man in his tracks, not anticipating these criminals were armed the man slowly backed away.

"Come on, we outta' here!"

The trio ran to the escalator in the middle of the floor, swiftly down they went with the brain leaving a trail of blood as they fled. It was little drops here and there, at first, seeping out from beneath his coat sleeve, leaking from his wrist, soaking his shirt cuff until it couldn't contain anymore, causing the excess blood to fall to the floor. The clothing disguised the fact that there was a lot of blood squirting from his artery. It was a little pin hole, a prick from one of the sharp spikes of glass that jabbed into his wrist when he reached for the watches; it didn't hurt, just stung. When he reached the first floor his adrenaline exploded, causing his heart to beat faster with each step he took, pumping his blood through the small, deep incision with ease.

After Pam was led to the security office in the basement, the guard was alerted by radio of the robbery. There was no alarm triggered when the glass was broken. The only sound was made by the culprits. After the guard made the lost child announcement, his walkie talkie crackled with the frantic screams of his female partner who was stationed on the second floor.

"Monty…Monty come quick! Dey' breakin' the jewelry counter! Monty, you hear me! Dey' robbin' the jewelry!"

"What's that Bertha…you say they robbing the jewelry?!" answered the guard at the front entrance who responded before Monty. He was the one in the best physical condition since Bertha and Monty were overweight, slow, and in their fifties.

"They broke the glass! They stealin' stuff inside the counter! I see um! It's three boys and one of um is holding a pipe!" She yelled as she ran toward the kids, panting, out of breath, slowing to a fast, paced walk, then stopping to suck in oxygen, unable to reach them in time to thwart their escape, all she could do was yell while pointing in their direction. Monty finally answered, "Bertha! Are they still up there? Which way did they go? Is they still up there?"

"Monty, make sure they don't get by you! You watch that exit good cause they gonna' be runnin' fast if they come your way!" the guard at the front entrance responded.

"But I'm not in the back! I went downstairs with the lost girl. You heard the announcement!"

"Get back upstairs! Call the police before you go! Hurry man!"

Monty called the cops as Pam sat next to him at his desk. He left her after quickly explaining the robbery, informing her she would be ok because the cops would also help her, when they arrived. As soon as he left Pam stood up, waited a minute and followed. The plan was for her to exit through the rear of the store but she decided against it because that's where Monty was going. No, she would leave through the front. She was smart enough to know not to run. She casually made her way to the exit amongst the crowd of shoppers scattering. Just as she reached the front of the store, she saw the young guard shifting from side to side with outstretched arms, ready to catch her friends if they approached, but they did not. Seeing the anger and confusion in his eyes, receiving a glare from him as she walked by, she proceeded anyway. He was unsure what to do but decided to let her pass because of her calm demeanor.

The three bandits headed toward the rear exit because the plan was for it to be unguarded since the security guard was supposed to be with Pam. They didn't think the guard would return so soon. They figured he would still be in the office with Pam keeping him occupied. To their surprise as they approached, Monty was standing in position and saw them.

"Yo'…. what's he doing there!" the lookout shouted.

"I see them Bertha! They in the back of the store. They were tryin' ta' leave and turned around when they saw me. You want me ta' chase um?"

"No Monty, stay put, secure that exit and make sure they don't get out. We'll keep them here until the cops come!" The guard at the front replied before Bertha could answer. She stood at the top of the escalator. There were three ways to get to the first floor; the escalator, an elevator, and stairs located on the north side of the building.

"What do ya' want me ta' do. I think they're still on the first floor. I'm by the escalator and they didn't come back up this way. I'm not sure if dey' came up by the elevator, or the stairs, I can't be in three places at one time," Bertha replied.

"No, you stay where you are. They're trying to leave. I don't think they would go back upstairs, there ain't no exits up there."

The bandits got off the main floor, which was white, smooth, slick, linoleum tiles with bright lights illuminating it. They walked against the wall, on the carpet, traveling through the accessories department, crouching low behind the displays, making their way to the front, unaware of the drops of blood that followed them.

"We gotta' get outta' here!" the enforcer exclaimed.

"Shhh, keep your voice down, don't panic, we got the watches. All we gotta' do is be patient and we'll get away," the brain replied softly. He was feeling light headed and loosened his grip on the duffle bag that was slung over his shoulder, noticing a drop of blood on his right boot as he did. His construction boots were tan, new, and he was upset. His friends saw the blood when he frowned and raised his toe for closer inspection.

"Yo' what's that? Looks like blood. Is you bleedin?"

"Yeah, I musta' cut myself on the glass. It don't hurt. It ain't that bad."

"I hear something…someone's coming…"

The boys peaked out from behind the counter where they were hiding to see Bertha standing about thirty feet from them. She was looking down at the carpet as she slowly walked closer.

"Where she come from? I thought she was still upstairs. What she lookin' at?" the enforcer asked, then looked down at the carpet too, only to discover the drops of blood that trailed them.

"Yo' she following the blood drops, dey' all over the place, yo' man, you gonna' lead her right to us," the lookout whimpered. He was nervous and didn't want to get caught.

"You gotta' stop bleedin'. We can't get away with you bleedin' like dat."

"There, take a scarf and tie it around my wrist tight. That should do it," the brain said, pointing to the accessories that sat on the counter top. The lookout was afraid to get it, not wanting to reveal himself, he stayed crouched on the carpet next to his friends as Bertha drew near. She turned her radio volume low and walked as softly as she could, unaware that she had already been spotted. The boys crawled along the wall now, moving from one counter to the next, concealed by the shadows until the carpet ended and they could see the front entrance, and the security guard, as he ushered out the last remaining shoppers.

"Damn, what we gonna' do now. We gonna' have to make a run for it."

"No, he'll catch us, maybe not all of us but he looks like he's pretty quick."

"Damn man, this was a stupid plan. You didn't think this out good. We gonna' get caught."

The boys were frozen in place, not wanting to retreat to the rear again, but realized it was their best option since the guard was older and out of shape, improving their chance for escape. The brain knew time was against them. He figured they only had moments before the police arrived. The female guard trailing them exacerbated the situation.

"You stay here. Imma' handle dis"

The enforcer was tired of being tracked like a wounded animal and decided to stop her. He would do what he normally did, use force and violence to solve his problems. Their eyes met and the brain knew what the enforcer was thinking, noticing him grip the crow bar tight, seeing the focused, certainty, that only brutality can bring, he didn't protest as his friend crawled away in Bertha's direction. The brain was growing weaker and because he was light headed from blood loss, he began to feel giddy and couldn't help but smile.

Bertha stepped onto the carpet after following the trail of blood down the escalator to the first floor's shiny tiles, disobeying her orders to stay upstairs. It was innocent really. She liked solving puzzles, and playing the game Clue, so these pleasures activated her detective instincts and compelled her to investigate further. She really didn't mean any harm. She was just going to alert her partners if she saw the boys. She had no intention of engaging them physically, because even though they were preteens, she knew her age and weight weren't an asset. No, she would only find them, if possible. She had no idea once she stepped onto the carpet that she was the one being hunted. The enforcer saw her studying the floor as she walked toward the accessory area. He looked at the blood trail too, and picked a good secluded spot next to the wall, by the drapes, and crawled under them, waiting. She arrived in moments, excited by the real game she was involved in, not noticing the drapes in this area were crumpled and disfigured, she was only concerned with discovery.

"What you smiling for. What's so funny?" the lookout wanted to know. He was nervous and didn't see the humor of their situation because there was none, but the brain was delirious as he slumped to the carpet and laughed outright now.

As Bertha walked past the enforcer's hiding spot, she heard the laugh and knew the boys were close. Distracted and focused on the sound, she didn't realize Willie was behind her. He crept from his hiding place and swung mightily at the back of her head with the iron crow bar only to have her duck at the last minute, which surprised him. It happened so fast she couldn't let out a scream, but she did gasp at the sound made from the crow bar cutting through the air. In shock from almost having her head crushed, she was unable to avoid the next blow. The enforcer smashed her in the knee on the back swing, aiming at a part of her body he was sure he could hit. Bertha did cry out this time but it wasn't piercing, like the pain, and she fell to the carpet, face down in agony.

"I told you ta' get that scarf and tie it round my wrist. You just a scare de' cat," the brain giggled. The lookout was too afraid to even peak from their hiding place to see if anyone was around.

"Look, here, you can use this," he said, undressing, removing his coat and sweater to reveal his white undershirt.

"Well… take it off then, and rip it in half, it'll tie better that way."

The lookout ripped the shirt from his body instead of pulling it over his head. He sat next to the brain and pulled his sleeve up to reveal the wound, only to be met with a spurt of blood shooting onto his bare chest. He instinctively put his finger on it as if it was a punctured soda can.

"Ohhh, that's a lot of blood. You see it squirting out…." the brain mumbled, growing weaker. "Move your finger. I'll put mine there, you get the shirt ready."

The lookout was so nervous he couldn't stop his hands from shaking. He was overcome with anxiety, fear, and being unable to contain his emotions he started to cry. He wiped the tears with the back of his hand leaving streaks of blood on his forehead.

"Awww, you're a big baby…it'll be alright. When I move my finger, you tie it tight, ok," he smiled, then moved his finger, but blood didn't shoot out this time, it just trickled while the lookout tied his shirt around the wound tightly, holding the brain's arm in his lap as they sat.

"I'm tired," the brain said, slumping onto his friend, resting his forehead on the lookout's chest, whose tears flowed freely now as he held the brain, he didn't bother to wipe them, they streamed down his cheeks, collected at his chin, then dripped onto the top of his friend's head. All he could do was sit there and hug the brain while he waited for the enforcer to return.

Bertha was in pain and couldn't walk, she couldn't follow the boys any longer, which was his plan, but she could still alert her partners to their location. The enforcer knew this and it was unacceptable. He had to finish the job. He had to make sure she wouldn't give away their location. He wasn't trying to kill her when he swung at her head, just knock her unconscious, thus solving their problem and the trio would have one less security guard to worry about. Willie raised his hands, griped the crow bar tight, ready to hit her in the head as she lay face down on the carpet moaning, when she rolled over to see the horrific sight of her attacker standing over her, about to bash her again.

"No.." she whimpered, "Don't do it. I won't tell. I won't say nothing," she moaned, and raised her walkie talkie, holding it out for him to take, halting his swing in midair. Willie had forgotten about the radio and snatched it from her.

"Das' right, take it…please… lawd' have mercy, you don't have ta' do it. Please father god, take the wheel, guide this young man right…please don't hit me no more son. I promise I won't say a word chil."

Her combination of begging and praying suppressed his anger, but still he had to be sure she wouldn't tell. He saw the terror in her eyes and was pleased. As she trembled on the carpet, he believed she was truthful, he believed she would be quiet. Her fear aroused him. Having complete control of a person, dominating someone like this made him feel superior. He liked the feeling so much he decided to threaten her. She needed to know he was serious. He frowned and formed his most menacing stare, then knelt down by her head and placed the pointed end of the bar under her chin, increasing the pressure while he spoke, until tears formed in her eyes. He drew his face near, smelling her lilac scented perfume as he whispered.

"If you scream or try to call out Imma' come back and poke your fuckin' eyes out…you hear me lady…you best believe dat," he ended with a sharp jab to her neck, never breaking eye contact with her since their noses were almost touching.

"Thank you, JESUS thank you, I won't say a word son, I promise…"

Willie crawled off in the direction of his friends. When he reached them, he was confused at the sight of the lookout, Charles, everyone called him Charlie, embracing the brain.

"What's going on," he whispered, startling Charlie, causing him to swing his head around revealing his blood smeared face.

"What happened? You bleedin?"

"No, it's not my blood. Where'd ya' git' dat' radio? You got it from dat' security guard? Whatchu' do? She didn't just hand it to ya'. Whatchu' do tuh' her?"

"I made sure she won't follow us."

Willie crawled to face them as Charlie continued, "He ain't doin' so good. He lost a lotta' blood, he tired, he restin' now."

Willie had seen dead bodies before and the brain had that same ashen complexion.

"He ain't movin."

"I know, he's sleepin."

"Let him go. Lemme' see."

Willie felt the brain's head, then he felt his chest, then examined his wrist, feeling no pulse, seeing that he wasn't breathing, he confirmed the obvious.

"I think he dead."

"No, what chu' talkin' bout'. He ain't dead. He jus' tired das' all."

"Hey fool look at him, feel him, you don't see him breathing do ya."

No, don't say dat', he can't be dead, not like dis', he can't die over sumthin' like dis."

Charlie was frantic now and crying too loud as he knelt next to the brain, rubbing his chest, mumbling to himself in disbelief.

"Shut up fool you gonna' get us caught."

"I don't care, he dead, he's gone, I don't care nuthin' bout' dat."

" I do. Gimme' that bag. I'm outta' here."

"You git' it yourself, I'm stayin' wit' him. We can't jus' leave him."

"I can….," Willie said as he slipped the bag off the shoulder of his friend's lifeless body, and crawled back towards the rear of the store passing Bertha again as she lay motionless. She closed her eyes tight when she saw him and whimpered, "Leave me be. I was quiet."

"I didn't come back for you," he revealed as he passed her, following the brain's blood trail, focusing on escape.

When he left the accessory department, the carpet ended and he crouched, staying against the wall. Seeing Monty guarding the rear exit made him feel at ease, since his appearance was feeble. Willie knew the security guard was no match for him, however, if Monty did put up a fight, he would bash him with the crow bar. Still, he figured a running charge wasn't wise. The element of surprise would be better so he stayed low, walking swiftly to the rear of the store, along the wall, holding the bag of watches tight, staying out of sight for as long as he could until he was unable to, beginning his charge on the guard's blind side from thirty feet away.

Sometimes you can tell when something bad is about to happen. You get a feeling of warning that overcomes you, making you cautious, and protective, this feeling caused Monty to turn just in time to see the enforcer's attack. Monty used to play football in high school, left tackle, so he instinctively got into his stance, blocking the enforcer with his upper body, surprising his adversary, causing him to fall back and drop the crow bar as he held onto the bag of watches. When Monty heard the clang from the metal hitting the floor, it startled him more than the running charge. It made him rethink his defense. He thought, 'Is this job really worth getting hurt for?' When he saw the crow bar his mind was made up. He didn't know if the boy had any other weapons but he knew street thugs carried knives. He wasn't willing to risk injury and backed away. The enforcer didn't attempt a head on charge again. This time he zigzagged as he ran by the guard unhindered, out the exit, and into the arms of the waiting police.

It was customary for the cops to cover all exits when responding to a robbery, so they were waiting with their guns drawn, since they knew the bandits were still in the store. Three police cars with six officers crouching behind their opened doors, called out to Willie over the loud speaker when he ran into their trap.

"Stop where you are, hands in the air, drop the bag!"

The enforcer reluctantly complied. He was shocked, and saddened, since he tried so desperately to escape. Once in his possession, he fantasized about purchasing extravagant things with the money gained from selling the watches. Naturally, he would go to the pimps and drug dealers. They were the only ones he knew with money, and would gladly pay for luxury watches since they enjoyed expensive things. To his misfortune, his dreams came to an abrupt halt as he slowly knelt, then lay flat on the pavement, face down, after dropping the bag.

Pam witnessed the arrest. She hadn't left the area after exiting the store. She waited nearby because she wanted to reunite with her friends and joyously travel home with them, and discuss their exciting caper, but she only saw the enforcer and wondered where the other two boys were. After the police handcuffed Willie and stood him on his feet, they questioned him to no avail, "Where are the others! How many are there inside! You hear me talkin' to ya' boy! An' suh' me!" one of the officers shouted, then punched Willie in the stomach.

Pam listened as the officer yelled at the enforcer. She walked closer and the police saw her, but they were unconcerned about a little girl and concentrated on their prisoner. She walked next to the wall, approaching the store again. She was close to the glass doors when four officers came running past her, entering the store. The other remaining officers placed Willie in the squad car before following their partners. His walkie talkie blared with an excited voice, exclaiming the news.

"We found um! We got two more boys in here! One of um' is dead! Better call for a body bag. The other one says it's only them, there's no one else, but we'll search the store anyway when backup arrives!"

Upon hearing the officer on the radio, Pam was astonished. 'Dead,' she thought, 'Dead, it can't be. How can one of them be dead? Who was it? I didn't hear any gun shots, what happened?' She had to know and followed the officer, staying back about twenty feet, not wanting to be noticed, easily advancing since Monty left his post and stood with his coworkers along with the police in the accessory department, as they hovered over the two boys. She crept upon them, crouching low, seeing the blood trail caused her eyes to fill with tears. The trail led her to the small group of men forming a circle, looking down at the carpet. She stood behind a display of handbags and watched.

"The ambulance is coming. You guys go and meet um' at the front and bring um' over here," said one of the cops who wore a white shirt while the other officer's wore navy blue. Two police men left and now the circle they formed had an opening, and Pam could see Charlie sitting on the carpet holding the brain in his arms. He was crying hysterically while the brain's head was slumped to one side, motionless.

Now the tears flowed from Pam's eyes too as she trembled in disbelief. Seeing the blood from the one she liked the most out of the crew, the one who excepted her into their family and introduced her to everyone, was distressing. Her heartbreak quickly turned to fear. She thought about her life and didn't want to die. She was afraid of death. There were many things she wanted to experience, therefore, she needed to be in a safe environment. Safety, that's what she desired now. Death was something she wasn't equipped to handle. She had no idea it was so close, looming over her, accompanying her daily. Her new environment was fun but it was too dangerous, since she could die or be killed at any moment. No, she had to get out, she had to get away from death, she knew what must be done. The thought of returning home relieved her despair. She believed a dull life with her family would save her.

It was a long journey on the bus returning from downtown Dayton. She didn't have the fare and asked the driver, while making a melancholy expression, if she could ride for free. He frowned but motioned her on, so she sat in the back by the window quietly crying, thinking about the friend she lost. When she arrived home, it was after eleven o'clock. The front door was unlocked as usual, so she opened it and walked inside to the surprise of Herby.

"Whatchu' doin' here?" he smiled excitedly. "You in trouble. Mama's been lookin' for you. Where you been? Mama! Pam's home! Mama you hear me!"

Ellen came running down the stairs as Pam closed the door. She heard the rumbling of footsteps before seeing her mother. The sound reminded her of playing on the steps with Baby Girl when they were little.

"Pam, my god your home!" Ellen screamed and rushed to her daughter, snatching her up into her arms, holding her tight for a moment, then pulling her away from her breast with extended arms to examine her.

"Is you hurt baby?" she asked as she moved Pam around from side to side, trying to see if there were any injuries, discovering none she held her tight again, then her joy and relief turned to anger.

"How dare you worry me so, runnin' the streets like dat'. You had me worried sick you crazy fool!" she screamed, and slapped Pam about the head with one hand while still hugging her with the other. She only stopped hitting her when she realized Pam was quiet and calm, taking the beating as if she deserved it, then she burst into tears, frightening Ellen.

"Oh no baby…. what dey' done to you? Lawd' have mercy. What dey' done to my chil?!" she screamed, looking to the ceiling, embracing Pam again as they wept together.

This was the beginning of a new chapter in the Hendrix family's life. At this moment everything started anew and all of the past memories were just that, memories. Ellen did her best but life was already in motion, and it's said that an apple doesn't fall far from the tree, however, in Baby Girl's case, maybe, just maybe it does.

About the author

I was born and raised in Mount Vernon, NY, in 1966. I always enjoyed writing and began composing songs at age thirteen, before that I only wrote essays for school assignments and was pleased by the positive reactions from my teachers and classmates. Growing up in the 1980's, attending Mt. Vernon High School from 1980-84, I won second place in a creative writing contest given by the Westchester Gazette in the non-fiction category, when I was 17, which resulted in my essay, "What Dr. Martin Luther King Jr. means to me," being published. I took the essay to the Black American newspaper in Harlem, NY, which is no longer in circulation, and was pleased when they also published it. I dreamt of being a star in the music industry but no record company would sign me so I decided to attend, The Center for Media Arts, in 1993. The school is no longer in business. I earned a certificate in Music Technology, then started my own record label, now defunct, "Allasia Records," and published my songs which can currently be heard on Itunes, Spotify, and all other digital platforms, under the name AY-D. This is my first novel and came about purely by accident. During the course of my life, I am pleased by the way technology made publishing easier for the self, publisher and independent musician. In the past it was expensive, and difficult to complete my musical recordings, and literary work.

Alvin Bernard Dunston
March 2019

BABY GIRL: Available on Amazon kindle edition, Barnes and Noble Nook, and all other ebook sellers. Search by Title & Author.

ISBN: 978-0-578-48872-1   Paperback
ISBN: 978-0-578-45879-3   Ebook

Contact information:

Ad10469@hotmail.com
Youtube: Alvin Dunston
Soundcloud: Alvin Dunston, Alvin D. James
Facebook: Alvin Dunston, Baby Girl
Instagram: Alvin Dunston
Itunes: AY-D
Spotify: AY-D

www.ingramcontent.com/pod-product-compliance
Lightning Source LLC
Chambersburg PA
CBHW071359290426
44108CB00014B/1614